The Social Market Found
The Foundation's main a
publish original papers b
experts on key topics in t
a view to stimulating pub...
markets and the social framework within which they operate.
The Foundation is a registered charity and a company limited
by guarantee. It is independent of any political party or group
and is financed by the sale of publications and by voluntary
donations from individuals, organisations and companies.
The views expressed in publications are those of the authors
and do not represent a corporate opinion of the Foundation.

Chairman
David Lipsey (Lord Lipsey of Tooting Bec)

Members of the Board
Viscount Chandos
Gavyn Davies
David Edmonds
John McFadden
Brian Pomeroy

Director
Ann Rossiter

First published by
The Social Market Foundation,
October 2005

The Social Market Foundation
11 Tufton Street
London SW1P 3QB

Copyright © The Social Market
Foundation, 2005

The moral right of the authors has been
asserted. All rights reserved. Without
limiting the rights under copyright reserved
above, no part of this publication may
be reproduced, stored or introduced
into a retrieval system, or transmitted,
in any form or by any means (electronic,
mechanical, photocopying, recording,
or otherwise), without the prior written
permission of both the copyright owner
and the publisher of this book.

Designed by Paula Snell Design

Contents

Contributors' biographies	4
Preface	9
Introduction	12
Putting the 'social' back into markets Michael Gove MP	21
Civic conservativism revisited Rt Hon. David Willetts MP	27
Healthy cities, healthy countryside Rt Hon. Oliver Letwin MP	35
Enterprise with a social purpose: the future of One Nation welfare reform Rt Hon. Sir Malcolm Rifkind QC MP	43
The consequences of state failure and the modern Conservative response Rt Hon. David Davis MP	52
Democratic renewal, national identity and social justice: a modern agenda for government John Tate	59
Conservative visions Rt Hon. John Redwood MP	71
Europe beyond Lisbon Dr Liam Fox MP	85
A new theory of the state and a new agenda for public services Nick Gibb MP	93
Better public services the modern Conservative way Damian Green MP	101
Direct democracy: a radical agenda for change Douglas Carswell MP	109
Raising standards: getting the basics right David Cameron MP	115
The failure of state centralism Greg Clark MP	127
Women, families and politics: the role of the state Andrew Lansley CBE MP	136
Principles of a Conservative economic policy George Osborne MP	141
Love, money and time: how to grow civil society Danny Kruger	150
Renewing the conversation Jesse Norman	166

Contributors' biographies

The Editor
John Tate read politics at Essex and Oxford universities before becoming Head of Research at the European Foundation, of which he is now a board member. As a senior consultant with McKinsey & Co. he worked in private equity and healthcare, co-authoring a landmark report on NHS reform commissioned by the Government. His policy publications include *The Children Left Behind*, *No Child Left Behind*, *Unskilled Labour*, and the *Drivers of Regulation* series. He is Chairman of a charity for the deaf, Chairman of the Associates' Club, and a school governor.

Michael Gove MP
Michael Gove has been a journalist since he left university, working for local and national newspapers, radio and television. A columnist for *The Times*, he has also appeared regularly on radio and television, including as a panellist on *The Moral Maze*, *Any Questions*, and *Question Time*. He is also Chairman of Policy Exchange, a centre-right think-tank. He was elected as Member of Parliament for Surrey Heath in May 2005.

Rt Hon. David Willetts MP
David Willetts is Shadow Secretary of State for Trade and Industry and has been the Member of Parliament for Havant since 1992. He was Shadow Secretary of State for Work and Pensions from 2001 to 2005, and has worked at HM Treasury and the Number 10 Policy Unit. He served as Paymaster General in the last Conservative Government. He is also a Visiting Fellow at Nuffield College, Oxford and a Governor of the Ditchley Foundation.

Rt Hon. Oliver Letwin MP

Oliver Letwin has been a Research Fellow at both Cambridge and Princeton universities. After working in a number of political positions in the 1980s, he went on to be Managing Director of N.M. Rothschild & Sons Ltd. from 1991 to 2003. Since 1997, he has been the MP for Dorset West. He has held numerous front bench positions and is currently Shadow Secretary of State for Environment, Food and Rural Affairs. Oliver Letwin is the author of a number of pamphlets, including *The Purpose of Politics* (1999).

Rt Hon. Sir Malcolm Rifkind QC MP

Sir Malcolm held continuous ministerial office for eighteen years, including as Foreign Secretary, Secretary of State for Defence, Minister of Transport, and Secretary of State for Scotland. He was the Member for Edinburgh Pentlands until 1997, serving on the boards of several major companies before returning to Parliament in 2005 as the Member for Kensington & Chelsea. He is presently Shadow Secretary of State for Work and Pensions.

Rt Hon. David Davis MP

A former Director of Tate & Lyle Plc., David Davis has been an MP since 1987 and since 1997 he has served as MP for Haltemprice & Howden. From 1994 to 1997, he was Minister of State at the Foreign and Commonwealth Office. In 2001, he was appointed Chairman of the Conservative Party, and in 2002 he was appointed Shadow Secretary of State for the Office of the Deputy Prime Minister. Since November 2003, he has been the Shadow Home Secretary.

Rt Hon. John Redwood MP

John Redwood was a company Chairman and an Executive Director of a merchant bank before entering Parliament for Wokingham in 1987. In the mid-1980s, as Margaret Thatcher's chief policy adviser, he helped her set up the then Government's privatisation programme. He later resigned from the Cabinet to make the case for rejecting the European Single Currency. He is a Fellow of All Souls College, Oxford and the author of several books.

Dr Liam Fox MP
Liam Fox is a General Practitioner and a former Divisional Surgeon with St. John Ambulance. He has been the Member of Parliament for Woodspring since April 1992. He was Parliamentary Under-Secretary of State at the Foreign and Commonwealth Office from 1996 to 1997, was appointed to the Shadow Cabinet in June 1998 and promoted to Shadow Health Secretary in June 1999. He has been Co-Chairman of the Conservative Party since 2003.

Nick Gibb MP
After a career as a chartered accountant at KPMG, Nick Gibb was elected as Member of Parliament for Bognor Regis and Littlehampton in May 1997. He was made Shadow Treasury Minister in October 1998 and Shadow Trade and Industry Minister in June 1999. He was on the Public Accounts Committee from 2001 to 2003 and on the Education and Skills Select Committee from 2003 to 2005. He was appointed as Shadow Education Minister in May 2005.

Damian Green MP
Damian Green is a former financial journalist and worked in the Prime Minister's Policy Unit from 1992 to 1994. Since 1997, he has been Member of Parliament for Ashford. He was a Conservative Front Bench Spokesman from 1998 to 2001, Shadow Secretary of State for Education and Skills from 2001 to 2003, and Shadow Secretary of State for Transport from 2003 to 2004. He is currently on the Treasury Select Committee and Chairman of Parliamentary Mainstream group.

Douglas Carswell MP
Douglas Carswell was elected Member of Parliament for Harwich and Clacton in May 2005. Before that, Douglas worked for the Conservative Party Policy Unit, having previously worked in investment management and television. Douglas stood against Tony Blair in Sedgefield in 2001 and has written extensively on the theme of direct democracy.

David Cameron MP
David Cameron was elected Member of Parliament for Witney

in 2001 and is currently Shadow Secretary of State for Education. He previously held posts including Shadow Deputy Leader of the House of Commons, Deputy Chairman of the Conservative Party, front bench spokesman on Local Government Finance and Head of Conservative Policy Co-ordination. He has also spent almost seven years at Carlton Communication Plc. where he was Director of Corporate Affairs and served on the Executive Board.

Dr Greg Clark MP
Greg was elected the member of Parliament for Tunbridge Wells in May 2005. He served previously as the Conservative Party's Director of Policy, responsible to the Leader for helping develop the Party's new policies. He also worked for the Boston Consulting Group and as the BBC's Chief Adviser on Commercial Policy. Between 1996 and 1997 he served as the Special Adviser to the Secretary of State for Trade and Industry, Rt Hon. Ian Lang MP.

Andrew Lansley CBE MP
Andrew Lansley has been MP for South Cambridgeshire since 1997 and since 2003 has been the Shadow Secretary of State for Health. From 1999 to 2001 he was Shadow Minister for the Cabinet Office and was responsible for policy co-ordination in the Conservative Party. Andrew Lansley was Director of the Conservative Research Department from 1990 to 1995. He has also been Deputy Director-General of the British Chambers of Commerce as well as a cival servant.

George Osborne MP
George Osborne was elected as the Member of Parliament for Tatton, Cheshire, in 2001. In September 2004, he was appointed Shadow Chief Secretary to the Treasury. He has also served as an Opposition Whip, a Shadow Work and Pensions Minister and Shadow Economic Secretary. He has been a member of the Public Accounts Select Committee and the Transport Select Committee. Since May 2005, he has served as the Shadow Chancellor of the Exchequer.

Danny Kruger
Danny Kruger is a leader writer at the *Daily Telegraph*.

From 2003 until the 2005 election he was a member of the Conservative Party Policy Unit, advising the Party across a range of domestic policy issues. He was Director of Studies at the Centre for Policy Studies from 2001 to 2005, conducting research into education, healthcare, economics and European policy. He read modern history at Oxford and Edinburgh universities.

Jesse Norman
Jesse Norman is Executive Director of Policy Exchange and a policy adviser to George Osborne MP. He studied at Oxford University and University College, London, where he is now an Honorary Research Fellow. He has worked at Kleinwort Benson and later as Director of BZW Ltd. He serves on the board of a city academy in Ealing and on the Advisory Council of The Roundhouse, a new performing arts centre in North London. He edited *The Achievement of Michael Oakeshott* and co-authored *Direct Democracy: An Agenda for a New Model Party*.

Preface

A lively debate is taking place on the future direction of the Conservative Party. The existence and good conduct of this debate were aided by Michael Howard's decision, taken in the face of much criticism at the time, to stay on and help facilitate it after the Party's defeat in May 2005.

Such a debate has never been more necessary. The Party's third unsuccessful election campaign, concentrating on five mostly negative priorities, persuaded just one extra person in every 160 to vote Conservative. Were the Party a public company, its share price would have risen by just 0.6%. Only if one takes the 25-year perspective can this be seen as anything other than a poor performance. Most of the eight million or so people who can be relied on to vote Conservative did so again and, in those meagre terms, the core vote strategy adopted by the Party's senior campaign managers succeeded.

Facing near-certain defeat, the Party might have used the election as an opportunity to present a new face to the public and thereby begin its rehabilitation. Broader, more positive policy messages could have been communicated on less trodden ground for the Party, such as the environment, poverty and transport. For all the criticism of his judgement and media performance, Iain Duncan-Smith had begun to do exactly this when his leadership was curtailed by false allegations of financial impropriety. While mocked as insincere, his focus on helping the most vulnerable in society found concrete expression in campaigns like that of his Shadow Education Secretary, Damian Green, on the American-inspired theme of 'no child left behind'. Mr Green's theme even won praise from *The Guardian*, while other projects broke new ground on the role of the voluntary sector. Shadow Cabinet members were dispatched to Denmark, the Netherlands, Sweden, and the United

States to learn about choice in health and education, vocational education, and other areas of public policy.

The policy directions taken under Mr Duncan-Smith were neglected in the run up to the last election as the Party switched from policy making to position taking. What the Party gained in discipline it lost in opportunism. Narrower, more targeted positions were taken on everything from scrapping the Human Rights Act to taking action against gypsy sites. It falls to yet another leader of the Conservative Party, then, to re-start the process of broadening the Party's message sufficiently to compete seriously for government. As Mr Howard himself put it in June 2005: 'we need to reach out; we need broad appeal, a programme that meets the many different challenges we face in modern Britain'. Vital to broadening the Party's appeal in this way is to augment its more traditional positions on crime, immigration, and taxation. To do, in effect, what Tony Blair has, in a fitful fashion, already done: give a human face to the new economic consensus forged under successive Conservative governments.

If these comments are so far too gloomy for Conservative readers, then they should find hope in the fact that the British people remain receptive to conservative policy messages. The public appear receptive to – or, at least, willing to listen to – conservative messages from their newspapers, radio talk show hosts, churches, and even, on occasion, from New Labour. (No doubt were editorialising allowed on British television then we would see conservative agendas emerging in that medium too.) So what is wrong with the Conservative Party as an author of conservative messages? There is no shortage of answers to this question. Not since George III has a patient received so many diagnoses.

Many cite the 'busted brand' argument: the view that the Party must be reborn, perhaps more radically than Labour under Tony Blair, to shed the perceived sins of its past. Others argue that if the Party is to win again then groups who would currently not think of voting Conservative need to be given a 'licence' to do so. To overcome their aversion to the Party these people need, on this argument, to see that it has something sincere and credible to say on issues that matter to them – an argument which brings us back to broadening the policy platform.

Still others argue that the Party's composition is the problem, with criticisms including that Conservatives are too old, posh, male, white, and tainted by past jobs in government.

Those looking for new people to take the Party forward can find hope in the 2005 intake of Conservative MPs, some of whom contribute to this book. As David Davis writes in these pages:

> The new generation of Conservative MPs [...] has shown a willingness to embrace radical new ideas and to learn lessons from abroad that should give us hope that the Conservative Party can once again come to the aid of those who are being let down by the policies of a Labour Government.

The leading members of a new generation of Conservative thinkers and writers – Douglas Carswell, Greg Clark, Michael Gove, Danny Kruger and Jesse Norman – have all supplied chapters for this book displaying ample intellectual vigour to power the Party's revival. Another hopeful sign is that so many credible candidates wish to apply for the Party's leadership – including, at the time of writing, many of the contributors to this book.

I wish to thank all of the contributors to this book. My thanks also go to my assistant editor, Ruth Farrer-Langton, who helped me with every stage of its development, as well as to Ann Rossiter, Director of the Social Market Foundation, who commissioned and guided my editorship.

John Tate, September 2005

Introduction

The Conservative Party has gone in a single generation from creating an economic consensus to ceding it to Tony Blair and his New Labour project. One of Mr Blair's principal opportunities was that successive Conservative governments had failed to create an adequate social emphasis to run alongside their economic reforms. The many social effects of embracing the market, from hard and immediate effects like industry restructuring to more general effects like rising individualism, were seen to have been ignored by the Party. Adding a social emphasis to the new economic consensus became the defining strategic opportunity for Tony Blair and New Labour.

The task of broadening the Party's agenda was finally taken up by Iain Duncan-Smith – but it had been left very late. The Conservative Party had become squarely associated with harsh and incompetent economic management. To lose this association the Party must indeed, as Mr Howard put it in June 2005, 'broaden its appeal'. The debate on the Party's future called for by Mr Howard is in no area more necessary than on the theme of this book: the interplay of civil society, markets and the state.

Recent Conservative policies have sent very mixed signals on the role of markets and the state. As George Osborne writes:

> Although we laid the foundation for the macroeconomic stability that Britain has enjoyed, we lost credit for it by voting against the Bank of England's independence. We have talked about reform of public services, but we voted against the creation of foundation hospitals. We have made theoretical arguments in favour of a smaller state, but in practice, we voted against tuition fees. We have consistently opposed strikes yet tacitly supported

the fuel protestors who brought England to a virtual stand still.

Mr Osborne's examples are far from isolated. Had the Party been elected in May 2005, patients could have combined their own and the state's money to be treated in private hospitals under the 'right to choose' policy. The same could not have been done for schools or universities, however, where co-payment would have been ruled out and rescinded, respectively. Britain would have promoted a robust line on economic reform in Europe and withdrawn from the Social Chapter, but would not have pushed for outright withdrawal from the largest subsidy regime in the world, the Common Agricultural Policy. Taxpayers would have been relieved of £4 billion in contributions from April 2006, but they would have gone on paying inheritance tax, 'pensions tax' and all the other taxes that would have seen the state continue to pocket around 40p in every £1.

Pragmatism is not new to British conservatism, of course. At the tradition's heart is a rejection of dogma and ideology, and a related belief that steering the ship of state requires a pragmatic captain. Thatcherism was exceptional in this regard, accompanied as it was by an unusually tight consensus on the importance of free-market economics. The dominance of this consensus, with its focus on efficiency and value for money, saw the Party in government neglect and even undermine institutions dear to most Tory hearts.

When under John Major the Royal Yacht Britannia was scheduled for decommissioning without replacement, John Redwood was almost the only senior Conservative to protest. 'Conservatives don't scrap the Royal Yacht', he said. Mr Redwood was also the only Cabinet Minister to oppose the Major Government's call for the closure of the 900-year-old St Bartholomew's (Barts) Hospital. In both cases, he opposed what he saw as the overemphasis many Conservatives had come to place on rationalisation and modernisation. While this emphasis was the result of an economic consensus forged by Margaret Thatcher, she like many Party members opposed the lengths to which it had been taken. As Mr Redwood remarked, Cambridge University was a similar age to Barts, and could easily be modernised with a new campus nearer the motorway.

The tight grip of the Party's new economic consensus had

reached many other areas of the state normally supported by Conservatives. These areas included the Armed Forces, which were subjected to successive rationalisations beginning well before the end of the Cold War, each of which brought deep cuts.[1] By signing the Maastricht Treaty, meanwhile, a Conservative government approved a transfer of powers abroad, to the institutions of the European Union, without parallel in modern British history.

While some traditional Tory concerns were neglected and even undermined under Conservative governments, another concern of far greater electoral significance was also neglected. Namely, the need to be seen to address the social effects of fundamental economic reform. While the neglect of more traditional Tory concerns like national sovereignty created room for the Referendum Party, the United Kingdom Independence Party, and numerous think tanks and pressure groups, the neglect of this social dimension created or significantly aided the emergence of a far greater pressure in the form of Tony Blair and New Labour.

A recurring theme in this book is how the Conservative Party can address itself – whether in health, education, political participation, or the built environment – to the more social side of the economic consensus it created. David Willetts argues that Conservatives 'cannot just be the economics party', but must also show that they understand the need for a strong society. Mr Willetts suggests some concrete measures towards this end, such as changing the tax code to support the family; doing more to recognise the role of grandparents in childcare; and offering impoverished communities greater financial stability through longer-term funding systems.

In my own chapter, I argue that the Conservative Party can advance social justice and national identity by better promoting the purpose and value of the nation state. Central to this promotion should be a radical programme of democratic reform, including a codified ('written') constitution and a wholly elected House of Lords.

Sir Malcolm Rifkind concentrates on the need for welfare reform, writing that, by focusing on the problems that perpetuate economic inactivity, welfare reform can become the key to sustaining high employment. Enabling 'a social market in

---

[1] Take for example the Royal Navy. At the time of the Falklands conflict in 1982, the Royal Navy had a small Fleet by her own historical standard, comprising 40 frigates, 33 submarines, fifteen destroyers, and three small aircraft carriers. By the time John Major left office in 1997, the Fleet comprised just eighteen frigates, nine submarines, nine destroyers, and three ageing aircraft carriers.

welfare provision' means giving private and voluntary organisations a far bigger role than at present. The Government's New Deal programme, far from 'creating' lower unemployment as Gordon Brown claims, has coincided with a slowdown in the fall of unemployment since 1993. Sir Malcolm shows how private and voluntary efforts to reduce economic inactivity offer better value and performance, despite recruiting tougher cases and receiving less state assistance. We must build on the success of private and voluntary welfare provision, he argues, while focusing employment-related welfare schemes squarely on skills development.

John Redwood writes that a truly social market is one that delivers plentiful employment opportunities to its participants, and that in this respect the European Social Model is profoundly anti-social. Liam Fox also writes on this theme, focusing on the EU's Lisbon Agenda and why its aim of making Europe the most competitive economy in the world by 2010 is unlikely to be met. He argues, like Mr Redwood, that the economic and regulatory reforms of Conservative governments have not been built upon, with the result that many other nations have long surpassed the competitive advantages Britain once enjoyed.

Mr Redwood uses detailed examples from medicine to traffic control to argue that over-regulation and high taxation reduce citizens' quality of life. Conservatives should commit to extend the 10% income tax band upwards, he argues, and reduce the top rate of income tax from 40% to 30%. It should also commit to abolish Capital Gains Tax on assets held for more than two years, he writes.

George Osborne sets out four principles of a new Conservative economic policy: macroeconomic stability, increased productivity, reduced demand on the state, and lower taxes. Establishing the credibility to communicate these principles effectively means resisting the temptation of opportunistic attacks on the Government; as he observes:

> Too often we have sacrificed long-term credibility for the prospect of winning the support of an aggrieved section of the population or the possibility of winning a vote in the House of Commons. Our short-termism has hampered attempts to develop a long-term economic policy.

Jesse Norman writes on the need to make room for the 'national conversation' often called for by politicians, particularly in the aftermath of the terrorist attacks on London in July 2005. Going beyond paying lip service to this concept requires, on his view, a radical enfranchisement of public institutions such as universities and local government – freeing them from their domination by central government. Institutional changes are not enough to facilitate a genuine national conversation, however, without a new emphasis on the importance of civility by which everyone is allowed to contribute.

Oliver Letwin writes of his belief that urgent action, local and national, is required to correct 'urban ugliness'. Success in this task would, he thinks, stem the exodus from the cities that is driving the over-development of the countryside. The action he prescribes does not mean repeating government-led mistakes of the past, but extending private and mutual ownership so that 'people feel a spiritual ownership of their surroundings'. It also means public authorities being more pro-active in encouraging businesses and individuals to beautify our cities.

Andrew Lansley considers the role of women in politics and public policy for the family. He makes the case for an 'A' list of Conservative parliamentary candidates containing many more women than at present, with winnable seats required to select from this list unless they have highly qualified local candidates. He further argues that the Party must understand families as they are and not as they were, given such trends as the rise in the number of unmarried couples, children born outside of marriage and children in lone parent families. 'Substantial government involvement' is required, writes Mr Lansley, to produce a simple and universal system of family support, including childcare, that is flexible enough to suit modern family life.

Danny Kruger writes on the need for political leadership by the Conservative Party to reinvigorate civil society in Britain. Central to renewing civil society is 'love, money, and time', by which he means promoting faith-based social action and stimulating a culture of private giving and volunteering. These tasks involve Conservatives facing two 'political imperatives': to localise and to moralise. 'Moralising' does not mean preaching from on high, he writes, but 'imbuing the Party's message with a moral motif and celebrating the compassionate instincts of the public'. Localising does not mean government abandoning its responsibilities, but 'taking more direct action to restore to the public their rightful power over the institutions which affect them'.

Nick Gibb and Damian Green, both argue that the Conservative Party needs to move away from allowing greater private sector involvement in health and education and accept that the state is capable of delivering excellent public services. The Party does not face a state sector dominated by failing corporations as it did in the 1970s and '80s, they observe, but one dominated by two core services – health and education – that the public have little desire to see privatised. International examples of excellent state-run services, writes Mr Gibb, include the Danish health service, the Swiss education system, and the New York Police Department. Internal market mechanisms fail, he continues, because they do not produce genuine market incentives and are overseen by politicians who, ultimately, will not let them fail. Both contributors agree that the Party needs to move on from placing more areas in the private sector and proceed with the more urgent, 'nitty gritty' task of determining how public services are best delivered.

Michael Gove considers how the Party can put the 'social' back into markets, arguing that Conservatives are – or should be – more the Party of Aristotle than of Adam Smith. Provision for female employees, childcare, environmental concerns and other 'non-balance sheet' issues should also matter more to commercial organisations, on his view. Some companies are 'slowly eroding the basis on which the liberal order depends', he writes, 'which is why it is not anti-market to encourage businesses to think more seriously about the work-life balance and review, for example, their drive to expand Sunday opening'.

David Davis writes of his belief that the Conservative Party must concentrate on transferring power from the state to the citizen. The modern Conservative Party must be willing 'to argue for the out-dated post-war consensus to be replaced with this new style of government fit for the 21st Century'. This new style of government means empowering individuals and, when this is not possible, their immediate communities. Mr Davis contests the argument, made by David Cameron in his chapter, that the Party has been too obsessed with structures, countering that new structures are the best way of raising standards. 'We should not advocate it out of blind ideology', says Mr Davis, 'but because giving people greater control of their own lives is the way to achieve the outcomes we all want to see.'

Greg Clark updates the theme of his 2003 book *Total Politics*, arguing that New Labour's obsession with targeting and central control undermines the quality of public services we receive. The Conservative response must be a radical programme of institutional autonomy – whether for schools, hospitals or universities – together with autonomy for the professionals who run them and the people who use them. The distinction between state and private providers must be broken down, writes Mr Clark, with state funding divorced from state provision and a better balance struck between local government spending and local revenue raising.

Douglas Carswell, in his chapter, shares Mr Gibb's view that the Conservative Party faces very different challenges to those of the late 1970s and 80s, and that it must therefore resist the temptation to continue trading on the intellectual capital of Thatcherism. Mr Carswell's prescription, however, is very different to Mr Gibb's: a radical programme of democratic reform pushing power down wherever possible to individuals and their locally elected representatives. The Party requires far more than a parliamentary majority to take on the left, he writes – it needs a method of breaking the left's grip on the hundreds of unaccountable institutions that now dominate public life. 'Direct democracy' offers such a method, writes Mr Carswell, with the capacity to end the lack of accountability that allows the left to impose its views by stealth – from the dogma of 'inclusion' in education to the liberal-left bias of the BBC.

Writing on education reform, David Cameron makes the argument, contested by David Davis, that Conservatives have talked too much about structures and not enough about content. The Party must now turn its attention to the latter, he thinks – in the case of education, to 'what actually happens in our state schools'. 'It is only once we have established what constitutes a good education that we should go on to ask: what stands in its way?', he writes. He calls on Conservatives to praise the success of Labour policy where appropriate; opening his chapter with just such praise. His theme of improving education content gives him ample ammunition with which to criticise Labour policy, however, including on provision for special needs and vocational education.

The reader will find that many of the contributors to this book, with important exceptions, share a desire to take powers back from the EU and to push powers down from Whitehall to individuals, their local communities, and their public service providers. A growing number of Conservatives seem to agree, to adapt Lord Ismay's formulation, that we must keep 'Europe out, power down, and the public in'. The new agenda of localism or direct democracy, and the ambition to give public service providers and users more power, creates a potent set of challenges and possibilities. The challenges to direct democracy are clear. Will a country with such a mobile and dense population accept the degree of local variation direct democracy could bring? Have British politicians the discipline to stop decrying all variation as a 'postcode lottery'? The potential advantages are similarly clear: voters become less apathetic as they are given more control over their immediate environments; unaccountable and unpopular policies are exposed and challenged.

There are further, often crosscutting challenges in pushing power down to individual schools and hospitals. As David Willetts observes:

> It is tempting [...] to go straight to the idea of each individual school and hospital being self-governing. Yet not all head teachers, for example, want to run their schools on their own. We must not fall prey to the cottage industry fallacy – imagining that the future of key services like hospitals and education is to be fragmented into tiny small producers. There are useful functions that can be carried out above the level of the individual school or hospital.

These comments point the way to the deeper policy debates that the Conservative Party must now have, going beyond simply handing head teachers the keys to their schools. Yet realising the vision set out by Greg Clark – where the distinction between state and private providers collapses as the former gain independence – remains attractive. Indeed, it promises services so diverse and innovative that their users will be astonished that they were ever all run from Whitehall. This approach of course raises questions as significant as those raised by direct democracy, but even more significant questions emerge when the two approaches are combined. What powers will be reserved for Parliament, communities, individuals and service providers, and how will the decisions to reserve them be taken? Who will prevail in disputes, particularly those between communities and independent service providers? Can a sovereign legislature ever refrain from reacquiring whatever power it gives? Or must Parliament itself be yoked by some higher law or binding constitution?

These are just a few of the policy debates that await the Conservative Party over the next Parliament. Whatever the future holds for the Party, the quality and variety of the contributions to this book show it to possess formidable intellectual breadth and depth. Harnessing these qualities to power the Party's revival will depend on combining the discipline established under Mr Howard with broader, more positive policy messages that reach beyond the Party's core support. This book will have succeeded if it can play even a small part in this process.

Putting the 'social' back into markets

Michael Gove MP

The great Austrian economist Friedrich Hayek believed in precision. This is why he distrusted the word 'social'. He believed it was a form of ideological anti-matter. It had the power to negate anything with which it came into contact. Prefix any worthwhile abstract noun with 'social' and the two would cancel each other out, leaving only nothingness in their place.

So, social democracy was the negation of true democracy, social justice did not lead to just outcomes and a social market was another contradiction in terms. Now, I know what Friedrich meant. Take social justice. True justice traditionally means due process, equity before the courts, rules which apply to all and the incorruptible rule of law. Social justice has traditionally meant demanding that the state step in to fix outcomes in life to address disadvantage, even if that means rigging the rules.

So a just admissions system to university just picks people with the best exam results, irrespective of where they come from. And a socially just admissions system would find out who was under-represented at university and positively discriminate to admit more from those groups. The demands of social justice, with its emphasis on more equal outcomes, run counter to the demands of traditional justice, which is corrupted by having one rule for one set of people, and another for a second group.

While I admire Hayekian rigour, I am not a pure Hayekian. Hayek himself wrote a famous essay explaining 'Why I am not a Conservative'. I am a Conservative, and as such do believe that there are goals which one can identify as socially just. Indeed, I would go so far as to say that the markets Conservatives should be in the business of defending are explicitly social markets.

Of course, the market itself is a quintessentially social construct. Buyers and sellers are not just categories in an economics textbook. They are roles which all of us play interchangeably in our lives, whether as sellers of our labour or our homes or buyers of goods and services. Our identities are, at least partly, defined by our participation in markets as homeowners, or renters, or employees. Markets only exist, and have meaning, through the free association of individuals who create relationships of mutual benefit. Much of the time we are participating in markets we do not even think of ourselves as economic actors but as social beings. We are in the local chemist's benefiting from the wisdom of the assistant as we try to find something to relieve our daughter's pain. Or we are in the office, collaborating with colleagues on a project which gives our day purpose.

A belief in a social market philosophy, however, goes beyond just recognition of the richness and complexity of human involvement in economic life. It involves a commitment to defending certain values which make it possible for markets to flourish in a civilised community.

Specifically, those of us committed to social markets believe that markets require a stable social framework, built on trust, transparency and liberal institutions, if they are to endure. We also believe that there is a responsibility on commercial organisations to respond to needs other than profit maximisation and shareholder value. Companies, especially big business, have a duty to think beyond the balance sheet.

The first requirement of social market policy-making is an appreciation that free enterprise does not flourish in a vacuum. Many of the institutions which keep the liberal order secure, and capitalism flourishing, are government's responsibility, from independent courts to honest tax collection. Yet there are other, deeper factors which help build the levels of trust and stability on which enterprise depends. Strong families provide the framework in which responsible citizens grow up. Family breakdown is linked to higher levels of criminality, welfare dependency and even absenteeism from work.

There is, therefore, a need for businesses to be aware of how their operations, in particular their employment practices, bear on family life. Do the hours they demand of employees reflect the needs of family life? Are they sufficiently flexible in the provision they make for female employees? Is sufficient value placed on the contribution parents make to wider society by raising children responsibly? Do employees, in particular women, suffer unnecessarily in their career when they make a commitment to family life? These considerations should be in the mind of every commercial organisation which respects its workers. They also matter, at a profound level, because commercial organisations which undermine the fabric of family life are slowly eroding the basis on which the liberal order depends. They are undermining the foundations on which their own prosperity ultimately rests. That is why it is not anti-market to encourage businesses to think more seriously about the work-life balance and review, for example, their drive to expand Sunday opening.

Companies also have a responsibility to think about the impact of some of their other activities on family life and our broader ethical underpinnings. Is it responsible for companies to use highly sexual marketing techniques when selling products to younger people? Is it appropriate for a company like French Connection to sell clothing to teenagers with an ad campaign based on implied profanity? Is it right that major recording companies should make profits from selling music which glorifies violence, the humiliation of women and defiance of the law? While any of these activities might be defended on the basis of giving the customer what they want, how appropriate is it to target teenagers in this way?

There are profound ethical questions involved here. A mature society, in which liberal institutions can flourish, depends upon adults recognising the importance of restraint and respect in dealings with others. Commercial activity which undermines those principles, and celebrates instant gratification, self-indulgence and empty hedonism chips away at the civilised structures on which we all depend.

As a Conservative, I am wary of legislation in these areas. Yet I do think that politicians can play a part in helping to start, and sustain, a conversation about business's responsibility towards society. I also believe that sustaining support for free enterprise in a democratic society depends on business proving it can act responsibly, otherwise the pressure for heavy-handed regulation and intervention will grow.

It would be far better for business, and those who believe in liberal capitalism, if commercial organisations were to show they understand their wider responsibilities, and frame suitably sensible strategies. Otherwise, the momentum will be with those who are, at bottom, opposed to wealth creation and wish to use business's failings as another stick with which to beat all capitalists.

In that spirit, there are other responsibilities which I believe business needs to consider, to show it is aware of the impact of its activities on other social goods. Our environment is, in every sense, a finite resource. Unless business shows that it is thinking seriously about sustainability then, again, it risks undermining the foundations of future prosperity and human flourishing. A commitment to the environment requires, however, more than imaginative thinking on energy use. It also requires consideration of the demands made by some companies for commercial expansion on greenfield sites and new housing for workers in already heavily populated areas. How is the quality of life affected by such developments? The countryside is not renewable.

Environmental considerations are not restricted to green fields. Commercial activity, particularly on the part of big business, is changing the ecology of our towns and cities. Major retailers, such as Tesco, are displacing smaller enterprises, homogenising high streets and eroding the diversity of Britain. Their procurement policies and approach to their supply chains

---

By putting the social back into markets, businesses can show that they understand and appreciate the importance of respecting the society which sustains them.

---

also shape agricultural production – not just in Britain but across the world, and often to the detriment of smaller suppliers.

The growth of several super-retailers, particularly supermarkets, may be a matter for inquiry on pure economic grounds, to see if their activities are consistent with maximising true competition and real choice. Yet, again, my instinct is opposed to regulation and in favour of more sensitive behaviour on the part of business itself. Too heavy a footprint risks bruising too many of our fellow citizens, and building up resentment towards a vigorous free enterprise culture. Respect for diversity and environmental balance is not just responsible behaviour in itself, it also builds trust between business and consumers. High trust societies are themselves environments in which it is easier and more pleasurable to do business.

By putting the social back into markets, businesses can show that they understand and appreciate the importance of respecting the society which sustains them. The more that we can show how businesses respect socially valuable ends, the more easy it is to use business's vitality, creativity and energy where it is desperately needed, in the provision of public services.

Advocates of social markets not only want to build support for enterprise by seeing it operate responsibly, they also want to see wider social goals achieved more efficiently by the use of market mechanisms. Public sector monopolies such as health and education are currently failing to deliver the quality of service the public deserves.

There is clearly a role for greater competition and pluralism in the delivery of these services. There is also, understandably, a public wariness that reform in these areas would lead to private sector involvement which would privilege the wealthy. It is also the case that the experience of some of the last Conservative Government's later privatisations, notably that of British Rail, has undermined public support for private sector involvement in the delivery of some public goods.

The development and deepening of a culture of social responsibility in business could make the process of involving the private sector in public service reform potentially more fruitful. Take the development of a social insurance model for healthcare for example. One of the principles behind the NHS which commands widespread support is the idea of pooled risk and social solidarity. The National Health Service is an engine of redistribution. Moves towards greater competition in health should respect that attachment to social solidarity by providing transparent mechanisms which show how new players in the market are helping the most vulnerable. Similarly, in education, new entrants to the sector should be invited to demonstrate their commitment to working with the most disadvantaged children first. That sort of thinking will come naturally to those companies or entrepreneurs who are already committed to acting in a socially responsible way. By helping, and encouraging, business to embrace social responsibility the ability of commercial organisations to help government achieve social goals is greater.

There has been a tendency among some on the right to believe that business discharges its social responsibilities when it sends off its tax bill. That seems to me to be a needlessly limited, and un-Conservative, approach. Conservatives have always seen business in a social context, and wealth creation as a means to an end, not an end in itself. Conservatives introduced much of the enlightened social legislation of the nineteenth century which governed how business operated and guaranteed an improvement in workers' quality of life. Conservatives have also incarnated the principle that with wealth or good fortune comes responsibility. The social stability on which the free enjoyment of property depends rests on respect for our fellow citizens.

Ultimately, Conservative politics is about the realisation of a good society. We are the party of Aristotle more than we are the party of Adam Smith. Economic growth is an immensely valuable goal, and a vigorous free enterprise economy the best way to achieve it. Yet economic growth is only one, albeit one of the most important, of the indices by which the health of society can be measured. Other values need to be respected alongside it; values that are the cornerstones of the stability and order on which a strong capitalist economy depends.

Civic conservatism revisited

David Willetts MP

Nearly eleven years ago, the Social Market Foundation published a pamphlet of mine entitled *Civic Conservatism*. My argument was that, whilst the free market was the exciting cutting edge of modern conservatism, it was not the full story. Conservatism stood as well for strengthening the civic institutions that stand between the individual and the state. Co-operative institutions and collective actions need not be in the public sector or instruments of the state.

This theme tied together our attempts to give more powers to local schools and hospitals. It also gave us a new way of thinking about crime, which was not so much individual selfishness out of control but often, especially with youth crime, more likely to be a deformed example of loyalty to the group. I also suggested that problems affecting us in the 1990s revolved around a deep uncertainty about how the family and the nation-state, the two most important institutions that stood outside and beyond the market economy, should take their place in modern conservatism. That was what lay behind the arguments about Maastricht and 'Back to Basics'.

Civic Conservatism was my attempt to contribute to a debate which really began under Margaret Thatcher. She became increasingly worried about the caricature that all she stood for was individualism, selfishness, and the profit motive. She laboured long and hard over her most significant attempt to respond to this challenge – her speech to the Assembly of the Church of Scotland in 1988. That was a very powerful statement of the obligation that we all had to our fellow citizens. But for her, as a devout and practising Christian, the answer to the question of our obligations to others was to be found in her religion. For her, the modern market economy was just putting into practice the parable of the talents; she believed that every individual should remember the virtues of the Good Samaritan. This was all true as far as it went, but it did not really solve the problem for Conservatives in a modern, secular society.

Resolving this problem remains the crucial challenge facing Conservatives to this day. We are still good at 'me'; we are not so good at 'us'. We are very good at the crucial importance of personal freedom and choice; we are not so good when other people come into the equation. We have to think about problems that require co-operation or obligation to others. This is reflected in the poll findings about what it is that still puts people off Conservatism. The public think that all we stand for is selfishness and greed. They think that we only want to help the well off. Well argued and well intentioned policies, for example for reforming the public services, are seen as just another device to enable the people at the top to opt out while others are left behind.

I am optimistic that we can once more make progress in getting to the heart of this problem. Few if any Conservatives now think that we can get by with the stale old argument that as we run the economy better we can afford to put more money into public services. The argument may be true, but it does not get to the heart of the matter. I always think that it sounds as if we are speaking through gritted teeth – like a divorced husband telling his ex-wife how much alimony he is paying her. Instead, we can learn from the explosion of interest over the past fifteen years in what has variously been called civil society, social capital, communitarianism, and most recently, for Tony Blair, the so-called respect agenda. The debate is so lively and productive for several reasons.

For a start, we saw the humbling experience of the reformers who tried to move Russia to a market economy after the collapse of the Soviet Union. They discovered that there was far more to a market economy than was described in the conventional economics textbook. For a market economy to work money had to be legitimate; there had to be understandings of what could and could not be done to out-smart your competitors. A modern market economy requires, in other words, a culture to sustain it.

At the same time, the evidence has been mounting about the family and its central importance. That old Conservative instinct that it is best for a child to be brought up by two parents within marriage is being supported by overwhelming empirical evidence. We also see the strong family not just as a way of raising children, but also as a robust heart of a wider civil society. A strong family can do many things for its members that in a weak and fragmented society end up having to be done by the state (which is why the cliché that social liberalism and economic liberalism must go together is so misleading).

Above all, it has become more and more obvious that this whole question of relationships that are not just about markets or the state is desperately important. The Chief Rabbi put his finger on the point when he observed, with typical wisdom, that what had really happened in the past twenty years was that both markets and the state had become stronger, and had encroached on everything in between. This might help explain why so much political debate is disconnected from the reality of people's experience. We argue on about markets versus the state when sometimes they appear to be allied in threatening so many things that we hold dear, such as the family or nationhood.

The interest in a civil society has even sparked some fascinating research into what exactly leads to the erosion of the time that we put in to our local community. Two chief culprits have been identified. First, the key difference between people who are active in their local community and people who are not is the amount of time that they spend watching television. Robert Putnam, in his book *Bowling Alone*, argues that it is the spread of television that above all has contributed to a weakening of society.[2] The second big factor is poor transport: every extra twenty minutes that you spend on your journey to and from work reduces the amount of time that you give to voluntary work by 10%. Clearly, if you leave work at 5.30pm and get home at seven o'clock stressed and exhausted, then you are much less likely to go out to the meeting of the Parent Teacher Association than if you left work at 5.30pm and get home relatively unstressed at six o'clock. One of the most beneficial side effects of a better transport policy might be more time for voluntary activities.

Tony Blair and New Labour did of course cotton on to

---

n, R: Bowling Alone:
pse and Revival of
Community (New
on & Schuster, 2000).

this debate. They are always sensitive to the ebbs and flows of academic research. Tony Blair talked about community, and academics were co-opted in to work at the Cabinet Office on an agenda for rebuilding Britain's social capital. But they failed. In fact, it is worse than that: this Government has done far too many things that have actively weakened communities and social capital. Clumsy attempts to require information on all the personal circumstances of those who just want to serve as parish councillors to be disclosed has reduced the willingness of people to give their time to this bedrock of the local community. Many reforms in education and health shared a complete failure to understand and value the professional ethos. The fiasco of the new Licensing Act is an example of exactly the phenomenon warned of by the Chief Rabbi. Big commercial pub chains are taking advantage of the new licensing regime to apply for longer hours at pubs. Meanwhile, the small local social club that might have had a bar in the corner to make a modest profit suddenly finds that the cost of getting an alcohol licence is now so extortionate that it gives up. This Government's notorious regulation and red tape is not just a threat to business, though that is bad enough, it is also a threat to local groups, charities, and professions. There is real opportunity here for Conservatives to develop our own agenda for making Britain's communities stronger. We cannot leap straight into policy, however, without having done a bit more hard thinking and research.

One of the latest and most insidious threats to local community action is the belief that the highest ethical standards must involve being completely detached from involvement in whatever it is that you are dealing with. It appears to have reached the stage where any local councillor who knows anything about his or her own ward is most unlikely to be allowed to participate in any decision about it. I do not know any other country which has taken its interpretation of public ethics so far as to require such disengagement by local councillors. People want to elect a community activist who will do something for the local community, but regulations force councillors to behave like Platonic guardians, unable to respond to local pressure.

Then there is the uncertainty that threatens so many of our localities. It is caused by government funding that always rewards the new project but fails to provide the stability and continuity for others. I see this on a tough council estate, Leigh Park, in my own constituency. We have had a host of initiatives over the past decade, each with their own acronyms and their own cheerleaders. Some of them have been very valuable – but they soon come to an end. Just when people feel that they are making progress, the funding stops. Then either the whole project is disbanded or it has to be dressed up to appear new in order to get to access some new source of funding. Reliable core funding for projects that work would be one of the best ways of providing what the voluntary sector really wants.

Then there is also the turbulence that comes from the fact that 80% of all the changes in local administrative boundaries within the EU take place within the UK. We are endlessly redrawing boundaries in pursuit of fairness or equity and, as a result, making it harder for good, solid, local representation to build up over the years. We can surely provide more stability in local boundaries without immediately degenerating into the gerrymandering so common in the United States.

We need also to establish, once and for all, where we Conservatives stand on the role of local government. Conservatives who speak up for local institutions and local decision making are often deeply uncertain as to whether local councils are the ultimate embodiment of the local community or are a threat to genuine local decision taking in individual schools, for example. There seems to be a political cycle here which all governments go through. What really angers Tories is when we see silly decisions by Labour-controlled local councils, intervening in what goes on in a school or college. You do not hear the same complaint so much about Conservative councils – and I am sure that is testament to the good sense of Conservative councillors. Yet there seems to be a process whereby whatever Party is in government loses ground in local councils. More and more of their own activists complain about the activities of local councils which are increasingly controlled by the Opposition, and successive governments find themselves taking more central control. It is time for a brave Conservative policy to break this cycle.

The most dramatic single move that would transform people's views of the EU would be if the European Commission were brave enough to admit that it had been wrong to take so many powers from national governments and that it was returning them to the democratic institutions from whence they came. Similarly, the most dramatic way that the Conservative Party could show that it was reversing decades of centralisation of power in Whitehall would be to take some significant areas of public policy and announce that they were going to be returned to local government. I increasingly see an opportunity to do this in the area of social security and welfare. Contributory social security is a national system based on standard contribution rules. Yet means-tested welfare is very different. Much of it used to be administered by local government. If a local authority is well run and has an effective social services department, why do we not give it the opportunity to deliver means-tested assistance to families? The obvious place to start would be the Social Fund. It is absurd that this discretionary payment is administered by the national benefits offices when it could easily go to the local authorities. You could then go further towards some Income Support as well. There might even be an argument for giving local authorities some scope for determining people's exact payments, within some central range fixed by a basic national benefit entitlement.

There is also scope for a really interesting and valuable Conservative debate about how public services could be decentralised. It is tempting, of course, to go straight to the idea of each individual school and hospital being self-governing. Yet not all head teachers, for example, want to run their schools on their own. We must not fall prey to the cottage industry fallacy – imagining that the future of key services like hospitals and education is to be fragmented into tiny small producers. There are useful functions that can be carried out above the level of the individual school or hospital. The Girls Day School Trust, which brings together independent girls' schools under a common umbrella, has been described as the ideal local education authority. It takes over functions ranging from administering the payroll through to architecture and building maintenance which schools have no desire to do for themselves. Both in America and on the continent of Europe we are increasingly seeing the emergence of chains of schools with a common identity ultimately run by a single organisation. On this model, deciding how to structure health and education looks like the debate on how to run a franchise. That means you have to be rigorous in defining the common features that give an identity to an organisation, and then defining where individualism and diversity should prevail. This debate is far more advanced in the business world than it is in the public services, and it would be good to see the Conservative Party being the first political party to enter it.

Finally, at the heart of a civil society is the family. We should not be afraid of quoting the overwhelming empirical evidence about the real impact that marriage makes as an institution. But we should not allow this debate to obscure our attention to the other big question – the importance of the extended family that crosses several generations. One of the biggest and most beneficial social changes over the past twenty years has been the increasing engagement of grandparents in the upbringing of their grandchildren (and yes we should be positive, social change can be good). Nearly two-thirds of grandparents now help with providing childcare for their grandchildren. The amount of money that grandparents give their grandchildren is not far short of the value of Child Benefit. Grandparents have very few rights, however. One set of grandparents told me of their distress when the parents of their grandchildren split up and they were told that now they were, in effect, ex-grandparents. Another report was of a parent who died and another parent who was unable to raise the children, as a result of which grandchildren were put into care even though their grandparents were willing to take legal responsibility for them. Surely, the reason why so many people are worried

---

Nearly two-thirds of grandparents now help with providing childcare for their grandchildren. The amount of money that grandparents give their grandchildren is not far short of the value of Child Benefit.

---

about Inheritance Tax is that they see the equity in their house as money that is going to be passed on to their grandchildren to help them get started on the housing ladder. Can we exempt transfers to grandchildren from Inheritance Tax? Can we tackle the pensions crisis by saying that assets put into pension schemes of relatives should be exempt from Inheritance Tax? These are options the Conservative Party should examine.

Conservatives believe in a flexible free market economy. We should never take that for granted. There is still much work to be done because our competitors abroad carry on raising their game. Yet we cannot just be the economics party. As well as being the party for a flexible economy, we should also show that we understand the need for a strong society. I have tried in this essay to set out what this means for Conservatives today. If we bring together our commitment to a flexible economy and a strong society, then we can once more place ourselves at the heart of British political debate.

Healthy cities, healthy countryside

Rt Hon. Oliver Letwin MP

Every year, 21 square miles of countryside, an area larger than Slough, disappears under new development.³ The Government's Barker Review proposes that the equivalent of 26 towns the size of Slough should be built by 2020. The character and tranquillity of rural Britain will be lost over a much wider area than the bulldozer's path.

Not even the once sacrosanct green belt is safe. In a recent response to a parliamentary question, the Government admitted that around four square miles of green belt are being built on every year. The Government claim to be adding to the green belt – and, indeed, they are: by expanding it on its outer edge, well away from development pressure, while stripping it away from the inside. Not so much a belt, then, but an elastic band that stretches as the countryside shrinks.

What is the response of the Conservative Party as the Government lays waste to rural England? We are out there manning our metaphorical barricades, shaking our scythes and pitchforks at the advancing army of bulldozers. It makes a huge noise locally, and the reverberations can sometimes be heard far away in Government.

Unfortunately, the bulldozers do not seem to care much. They are hardly dented, much less arrested. So the destruction goes on, and the countryside shrinks. Soon, southern England⁴ will be one large, landscaped housing estate – with the odd car park, posing as a motorway, thrown in. Clearly, our tactics in opposing this development do not seem to be working.

Why not? The straight answer is that the metaphorical

barricades will not stop the bulldozers because they cannot stop the market demanding more suburban dwellings. If we want to do anything constructive and effective about the problem, we have to understand its cause. And, once we start looking seriously for the cause, it is not hard to find.

The pressure of development on the countryside has one overwhelming cause: the exodus from the cities. According to the Halifax, in the ten years to 2003, over two million people left London – mostly for the suburbs, towns and villages of southern England. Others take their place, of course, from other British cities and from abroad. And, in time, many of these will also join the exodus into the countryside – a flow of humanity which compares with the great migrations of history.

Yet what drives people out from the city to the country is not death, war, famine or pestilence, but that fifth horseman, ugliness – which may take many forms: the physical threat of crime and anti-social behaviour; the mental stress of a dirty, noisy congested environment; the spiritual deprivation of a daily routine unrelieved by glimpses of urban beauty.

The urban rich isolate themselves from this ugliness by buying themselves into elevated positions – often quite literally. From the penthouse canopy, the concrete jungle does not look so bad. In fact, when lit up at night it is quite fetching and the streams of traffic all the more so. That does for the weekdays. And, at weekends, when they might otherwise be forced to confront the reality on the ground, the urban rich escape to the countryside – in second homes which price local country people out of the housing market and progressively undermine rural life, turning once thriving village communities into dormitories.

The middle classes cannot afford the penthouse or the country cottage, but they can get out – to the expanding suburbs and commuter towns. As they move out to the suburbs, the green belt comes under strain and, notch by notch, is loosened by Government policy.

Finally, there are the least advantaged who are stuck where they are. They suffer a spiral of decline. The more the middle classes move out, the less money there is to invest in local businesses or the improvement of property. Council revenues fall, leaving local authorities with less money to invest in public spaces. There is a further deterioration in the local environment, and yet more of those who can leave do so, trapping those who cannot leave in a vicious circle of uglification.

Urban ugliness affects different people in different ways. But the losers are the countryside and the least advantaged city-dwellers. This is environmentally and socially unsustainable.

The lesson is clear. If we want to preserve the countryside, instead of fighting a losing rearguard action to keep the second-homers and the suburban bulldozers at bay, we must make our cities places where people want to live. Of course, there will always be those who want a rural way of life, just as there will always be those who will move to the city. Yet, for many, ugliness is a price not worth paying despite all the other advantages of the city. Change the equation by making the city more beautiful, and many will make a different decision.

Urban beauty is neither unprecedented nor impossible. So how do we make our cities as beautiful as any in the world? First, we must realise that the heavy hand of government building and re-building is not the solution. Look at our cities. Look what governments built. A lot of it is not pretty. A lot of it does not seem to be built with people in mind. Once the architects have gone away, it is the people left behind who make the difference. If they live in state-built buildings that lack the human touch, will they pick up the litter or drop it? Will they mend the windows or break them?

One of the great lessons of the 1980s was the huge improvement in the urban environment that could be created in places where people exercised their right to buy on a large scale – different ownership patterns generated different attitudes, and a new pride in places generated a new look to places. That is why the Conservative Party was right at the last election to talk about an extension of the right to buy – and why we would be right in the next few years to think through the opportunities for mutualisation of ownership in areas where private ownership cannot be extended. If we want to see the urban environment improved, there is nothing we can do which is more important than giving urban communities a sense of ownership of their surroundings.

Yet the responsibility for the beautifying of the urban environment is a shared one. Government, too, has to play a continuing role. This is especially true of the public spaces that bind together the private places of a city. As individuals, we have neither the incentive nor the resources to beautify whole townscapes and parkscapes – not when we struggle with our own homes and gardens. And even the very rich, who might have the money, and, just possibly, the inclination, do not have the power. After all, there is no point in creating a park if someone else can build all over it.

Public spaces require public action. Just as the great parks of our great cities were once founded by public agencies, so, now, our public spaces must be improved and maintained by the public authorities. It is only the public authorities that have the cash and the power to do what is in the interests of all the citizens but not in the interests of any one citizen.

And this further action to improve and beautify public spaces has to go right out to the peripheries – deep into the poverty belt that surrounds so many of our city centres. In the words of the Bishop of Liverpool, there is a:

> Real danger that…our cities could fall sick with…urban diabetes…that is, the blood pumps around the heart of prestigious city-centre projects but fails to get to the extremities of the body…these parts of the city then wither and die.

The Bishop is right; the lifeblood of beauty must pump round the whole body – not just to the downtown loft dwellers, but to every community across every city. If restricted to the geographical centre, or to the centre of power, urban regeneration will fail.

At present, many of the public spaces in our cities are run down rather than kept up. They diminish, rather than enhance, the quality of life. They dishearten rather than inspire the private citizens seeking to beautify their own patches. Too often, there is a sense that the whole apparatus of urban planning is reactive, prohibitive, negative and that pro-active efforts to improve the green spaces and the street scenes are limited, lethargic and timid. But even when improvements are made to the urban public spaces, all too often private business leaves a remaining blot on the landscape. One city street I am familiar with – I shall not name the street or the city – is an example in this respect. Over the years, the local authority has considerably smartened the road surface, the pavements, the street lighting. Aesthetic improvements have run in parallel with refurbishment, both of the blocks of flats and of several of the business premises. The street is 'on the way up'. Yet the whole environment is let down by a car park that is ill-maintained, with tumbledown fencing, piles of rubbish and ill-assorted shacks, and by a small patch of ugly, concrete wasteland that has lain empty for ten years.

Here is a classic case of shared responsibility: the public authority has done its bit for the public spaces; individuals and some of the businesses have done their bit for much of the private space. Surely, we need to find some means for the public authority to induce the remaining private businesses to do likewise for the common good.

An example of the way in which the private and the public can work together to achieve the common good of urban regeneration is the town of Bar-le-Duc in northeastern France. The town and its buildings are old and, thirty years ago, they looked in near-terminal decline. The stonework was filthy with years of grime; the masonry was crumbling; paint flaked from windowsills; and shutters hung off their hinges. It was a scene of decay more at home in the Balkans than in Western Europe.

Fortunately, the town council decided to make a difference. Public buildings were cleaned up and people saw just how beautiful their own houses might look, so there was no real opposition when the council required all property owners to clean the frontages of their homes and offices within five years. As an added touch, there was a further requirement to re-paint shutters and windowsills within a given palette of colours based on the town's coat of arms.

These methods might seem just a little too regulatory to us. Yet the result was – and is – stunning. Beauty had returned to Bar-le-Duc, as did much of its former population. Abandoned buildings were restored, along with a medieval market that now does a thriving trade after centuries of disuse. Restaurants have opened and local shops are back to stay. Property prices are up, but not outrageously so – because regeneration pervaded the whole community, not just privileged enclaves. The process of beautification goes on. Not at the behest of the council, but because of local pride – everyone now wants their home to look as good as their neighbours'.

Bar-le-Duc is no Paris commune, just an unremarkable corner of everyday France. People get on with their own lives, in their own homes, minding their own business. Yet, by creating the right conditions, authority as an expression of community has allowed individual interests to work for the public interest.

To recap, my argument so far is simple. First, our countryside is being eaten away by the bulldozers and our rural communities are being eaten away by second homes. Second, there is no point in hoping that we will stop, or even substantially impede the process by rural protest, because the pressure for suburban and rural development is caused by a mass exodus from the cities of all but the disadvantaged. Third, the exodus from the cities is driven by urban ugliness and the conditions of life that such ugliness fosters. Fourth, if we are to save the countryside, we have to find effective means of making our cities more beautiful. Fifth, this does not mean repeating the mistaken public sector building projects of the past; on the contrary, it means extending private ownership and mutual ownership so that people feel a spiritual ownership of their surroundings. Sixth, it also means the public authorities paying far greater attention to the quality of public spaces. Seventh and finally, it means public authority more pro-actively encouraging private business and private individuals to play their part in a common enterprise to beautify the city.

Now we come to the really difficult bit. If we are to save the countryside by beautifying the cities, and if this involves, among other things, public authorities pro-actively encouraging private business and private individuals to play their part in a common enterprise to beautify the city, how do the public authorities achieve this goal without excessive nannying and collateral social and economic damage? What is the recipe for achieving the Bar-le-Duc effect on a much wider scale?

One cannot answer this question in a single essay; indeed, nor can a single politician. I shall rest content if my argument creates a debate about how we can foster a sense of shared responsibility for urban regeneration – especially if that debate recognises also the vital role urban regeneration has to play in saving our countryside. I will, however, provide at least a few pointers towards what seem to me the most fruitful avenues of exploration, when it comes to the role of public authorities in fostering a sense of shared responsibility for urban beautification.

The most obvious point, I believe, is the need to adopt what I have previously described as an attitude of thoroughgoing localisation. The ugliness of much of our urban environment, and the destruction of much of our countryside that is driven by the consequent urban exodus, is a national problem and one that our national government cannot afford to neglect. Yet the solution to the problem must be local, not national, because it must be based on a profound and detailed understanding of place and of the desires, habits and concerns of those who live in that place.

Accordingly, I do not believe that there is much hope of achieving the desired urban transformation through yet more, highly specific, national schemes. Schemes, rules, performance monitoring, reports, evaluations, committees and the like tend to be the enemies rather than the friends of progress as far as urban regeneration and beautification are concerned.

What is required, rather, is a willingness on the part of central government to take more on trust – to take more risk: to provide local public authorities with more power and rather more access to unconstrained funds; to augment, rather than to

---

The ugliness of much of our urban environment, and the destruction of much of our countryside that is driven by the consequent urban exodus, is a national problem and one that our national government cannot afford to neglect. Yet the solution to the problem must be local, not national.

---

diminish, the role and standing of locally elected representatives; to foster in as unconstrained a way as possible participation by local businesses; to lead by rhetoric the establishment of a national sense of shared responsibility for the urban environment; but to avoid the imposition of targets, the issuing of directives and central intervention.

In short, whilst the question is national, the answer is not. We need, as a nation, to ask how we can achieve a consciousness of shared responsibility for our urban environment. We need, as a nation, to set a framework that allows and encourages urban communities and urban authorities to take such shared responsibility. This is the only way in which we can at one and the same time enhance the lives of the least advantaged urban dwellers and save our countryside from what is otherwise bound to be a continuing exodus of the more advantaged. But we need to recognise that the answer to the question – the specific action within the framework – cannot be formulated at national level. It has to be formulated locally and in response to the particularities of local circumstance.

The health of our nation, and hence the health of our countryside, depends on achieving a culture of shared responsibility for urban aesthetic renewal which is national in scope but local in form.

Enterprise with a social purpose: the future of One Nation welfare reform

Rt Hon. Sir Malcolm Rifkind QC MP

I am proud to have served in a Government that introduced the reforms necessary to allow increasing numbers of people to move off benefits and into work. Until recently, unemployment had been declining steadily since 1993, but now that trend has stalled and a growing hard-core of people are being left behind by rising prosperity.

Many of these people have fallen into long-term unemployment, just because they lack the basic skills employers need. Others face difficult barriers to work, such as sickness, disability, or because they bring up children on their own and cannot get decent, affordable childcare. It is saddening that they are often seen as somehow divorced from the rest of society. Mr Blair has even described them as 'an underclass of people cut off from society's mainstream without any sense of shared purpose'.[5] We should not accept that.

In fact, most of these people play a very active part in their local communities, minding the children of friends and relatives, working as volunteers, or simply looking out for their elderly neighbours. These people must never therefore be written off to languish on benefits. Yet in order to give them the right kind of help, we must break new ground with fresh thinking on welfare reform.

Some people think that introducing market choices and mechanisms into the delivery of social services is anathema to the principles upholding the welfare state. Yet throughout the country, independent commercial and voluntary sector organisations are proving them wrong. Every year, enterprising companies with a social purpose are helping tens of thousands of people overcome their problems and turn their lives around. That is why we must harness much more of this local expertise, allowing it to benefit everybody, not just the few. But for more radical improvements, we need to go even further.

We need to take a fresh look at the very purpose of welfare provision. The job of responsible government is to help people free themselves from dependency, so simply telling them to find work is not enough. There are in fact hundreds of thousands of jobs available at any one time, and many more would appear if our labour supply were in better shape. The welfare state could therefore play a far more effective role if only it helped unemployed people gain the skills employers need to fill these vacancies.

This essay envisages a modern, One Nation framework for welfare. This would combine business excellence in service delivery with a strong social purpose, to give people the tools they need, not just to find a job, but also to achieve lasting financial independence for themselves and their families.

Any such case for reform must begin with strong, unequivocal evidence that demonstrates the need for change. As well as large numbers of people being left out of the labour force, we can clearly see that the people who face the most stubborn barriers to work are not receiving the right kind of help. In order to illustrate these problems, I want to first point out some important labour market trends.

Labour often claims that falling unemployment is due to the success of its own policies, especially the New Deal unemployment programme. However, official figures show this cannot be the case. The graph below shows unemployment was falling steadily from 1993, and that when the New Deal became operational in 1998, the rate of decrease actually slowed.

The job of responsible government is to help people free themselves from dependency, so simply telling them to find work is not enough.

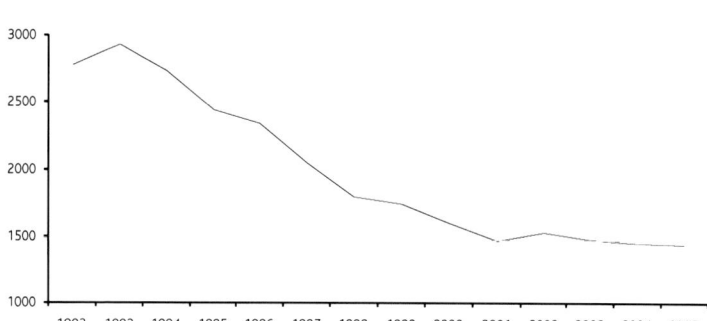

Unemployment in the Working-Age Population 1992-2005[6]

(Introduction of New Deal = 1998)

Not only did unemployment start falling years before the current Government took office but, since the beginning of Labour's second term, there was no real improvement in the employment rate. By the beginning of 2005, the Office for National Statistics observed that, 'the more recent rate of increase has been no more than in line with population growth, leaving the real trend in the employment rate largely flat since 2000'.[7]

In the light of such figures, it is clear we need to focus more closely on why there are large numbers of people of working age who want a job, but are not working. At the time of writing, the 2005 unemployment figure stood at over 1.4 million people, of whom 865,000 were claiming Jobseeker's Allowance benefits. In addition to the officially recognised unemployed, however, there are increasing numbers of people who do not appear in the official unemployment count. They are defined as 'economically inactive' or 'incapacitated'.

There are eight million working-age people in the UK defined as economically inactive. They include the disabled, homemakers, students, and people who simply do not want a job. But according to the *Labour Force Survey*,[8] two million of these people say they do want to work, yet are not counted as officially unemployed. They are often lone parents who cannot work for want of childcare, or people trying to get back on their feet after sickness or personal difficulties, or those who simply do not know how to start looking for a job. There are also 2.7 million working-age people on Incapacity Benefit, claims for which have risen by 140,000 since 1997.[9] Of course, many claimants are afflicted by serious sickness or disability and cannot work. However, many of them can – even Labour admits that at least a million claimants are willing and able to work.[10] The Shaw Trust charity puts the estimate even higher, at 1.5 million.[11]

In the last year alone, paying and administering the main out-of-work benefits and employment programmes for all of these different groups cost some £20 billion, as illustrated below.

The Cost of Unemployment 2004-5[12]

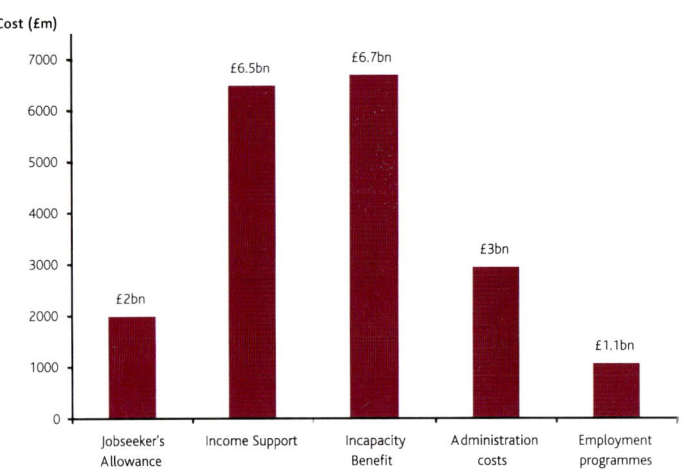

This figure actually underestimates the true cost of unemployment, as it does not account for the fact that recipients of out-of-work benefits often claim other general benefits, such as Housing Benefit and Council Tax Benefit. The human cost of failing unemployment programmes is, of course, far greater. Sadly, current policy does not provide effective help for people facing serious disadvantage and personal difficulty. Existing schemes target the easiest to employ, at the expense of those who really need help.

The Government's principal policy for tackling long-term unemployment is the 'New Deal'. The official statistics show that of all the over two million people who have gone through New Deal schemes so far, less than a third have moved into what are called 'sustained jobs', defined only as work lasting more than thirteen weeks.[13] Official reports even state that of the minority of people finding work through the schemes, most would have done so anyway, fuelling a large deadweight cost.[14]

The Government has also attempted to reduce the numbers claiming Incapacity Benefit, and in 2000 tightened up the rules for claiming and added a means test. Yet this resulted in the claimant figure rising from 2.6 million to the current 2.7 million. Claimants were put off leaving Incapacity Benefit for fear of not being able to return to it if they became sick again. Now, further reforms have been announced which involve separating out those claimants deemed more able to be helped back to work and pushing them through the failing New Deal.

Current policy lacks direction, quality and focus. People with complicated personal problems simply do not get the level of service they need because DWP targets lead advisers to concentrate on the easiest cases, placing those who are already the most job-ready. Government schemes do not target people's employability enough, so those with little or nothing in the way of skills end up in long-term benefit dependency. The result is that billions of pounds have been pumped into programmes with very limited success. The contrast with the many locally based enterprises and voluntary organisations that help people into work could not be starker.

The organisations that are best at helping the unemployed and disadvantaged into work have one thing in common: they use business excellence to champion a social purpose. Independence from government allows them to focus on how best to achieve lasting results for people, rather than negotiating Whitehall targets. People trust them because they have their best interests at heart.

Take the Shaw Trust, for example. They grew from a tiny charity based in a small Wiltshire village into the largest provider of employment services for disabled people in the UK. They also help many others who are disadvantaged by ill health or personal problems. Last year, the Shaw Trust helped over ten thousand disabled and disadvantaged people into work, and expects to place another ten thousand this year. They also really know their clients' needs – one in five Shaw Trust staff is disabled.

Another example is Tomorrow's People, a trust which

grew from small beginnings into a nationwide provider of back-to-work help for unemployed people with difficult personal problems, such as homelessness or addiction. Despite the fact that Tomorrow's People take on much tougher caseloads, they are better than the New Deal at placing people into work that lasts – and do so more cheaply. This is illustrated below:

Comparison of schemes: New Deal vs. Tomorrow's People[15]

	New Deal	Tomorrow's People
Percentage of leavers who move into work	40	43
Percentage of leavers who find work lasting more than thirteen weeks	32	40
Gross cost per new job created	£3500	£2050

Furthermore, many of the people who do not find work through Tomorrow's People still achieve a positive outcome. In addition to the 43% who find work, another 13% move into education, training or voluntary work. A recent review conducted by Oxford Economic Forecasting stated that over their twenty years in operation, Tomorrow's People alone have saved the exchequer £450 million.[16]

In addition to such charities working alongside government, there are several commercial firms and not-for-profit organisations that deliver employment services under contract from the Government. The most notable have been in 'Employment Zones', which, though placed in the most depressed labour markets, consistently produce better outcomes than state-run New Deal schemes.

The reason these independent providers are giving people more effective help, even though they spend less and take on harder cases, is because they are specialists. They understand the needs of their clients and have the expertise to deal with them. They also have an in-depth knowledge of the needs of local employers, and which companies are more amenable to

15 Source: *Twenty-Year Evaluation of Tomorrow's People*, Oxford Economic Forecasting, September 2004.

16 Ibid.

taking on people with personal difficulties or disabilities.

The state just does not provide this quality of service – and so it should step aside and provide the funding for others who can. A greater role for the commercial and voluntary sectors would not only mean opening up the capacity for quality and choice in welfare services, it would mean higher numbers of people could be helped back into work.

The Conservatives rightly went into the 2005 election proposing to expand on the amount of services that are contracted out to independent providers. Our policy was to fund independent specialists from the commercial and voluntary sectors to run job centre services. But if we really want to improve welfare, we should attach a much stronger and more dynamic purpose to its provision.

The way forward for welfare reform is to combine business excellence in service delivery with a national strategy to raise skills in the least employable. This means using local enterprise to help people gain the skills they need to sustain financial independence in the long term.

There were 640,000 job vacancies in the UK at the time of writing,[17] and the Government's own research shows that shortages of intermediate skills amount to around £10 billion in lost business potential annually.[18] This means that even more jobs could be created if employers were presented with a better quality labour supply. Indeed, there is clear evidence that employers in the UK are increasingly demanding higher skills on job entry. The annual National Skills Survey,[19] for example, shows that even in lower-level service and production jobs, which people coming off benefits tend to move into, a basic degree of literacy, numeracy and computer competence is becoming an increasingly standard requirement.

All the evidence demonstrates that the higher a person's skills, the lower their risk of unemployment. If unemployed or 'inactive' people could be made available for work with decent basic skills, not only would they have better life chances, they could support the British economy in reducing skills gaps.

We must make sure, however, that we do not simply produce slightly better qualified, but still unemployed people, and we cannot simply engineer the skills we think employers want. That is why we must let employers take the lead. We need to deliver services through commercial and voluntary sector contractors who know the needs of the local economies they operate in best. Independent providers from the commercial and voluntary sectors should be paid to run our labour market programmes and, when necessary, should be able to purchase for clients the training directly relevant to local employers' needs. This could mean anything from a short computer course to a national vocational qualification, to a licence to operate a chainsaw. In effect, the market would show the way.

Such reform cannot be achieved without a cost, and it may be argued that individuals or employers should themselves foot the bill for the skills they need. On the whole, I would agree. However, in the case of the long-term unemployed or sick, most employers just do not have an economic incentive to provide such a level of pre-labour market training, and most unemployed people lack the resources to invest in it themselves. In any case, the main benefit of a skills development role in welfare is that it would reduce the deadweight cost inherent in so much current policy.

We must be mindful, however, not to continue mistakenly concentrating only on the cost of policies at the expense of their *value*. Helping an older ex-steel worker, for example, who believes his industrial experience is obsolete in the modern workplace, learn a new set of skills and build the confidence to get a job has an intrinsic value far in excess of any money the state saves in his benefits. Helping a lone mother into work not only re-engages her with the labour market, it allows her to show her children the benefits of earning an independent income.

Of course, training should only be provided where it is absolutely necessary. For people who simply lack motivation, a nudge in the right direction will always be best, and there is a role for compulsion to enforce work attachment. For sick people, purchasing rehabilitation may take precedence. For lone parents, childcare arrangements may need to be put in place. The point is that the power of choosing what is best for each case is put in the hands of the unemployed person and their local service provider.

One Nation welfare reform, as the essay describes, harnesses the dynamism of enterprise and channels it towards helping everybody gain the skills they need, not just to find a job, but also to achieve the independence of a lasting career. It involves:

- revitalising welfare-to-work by making it part of a national strategy to raise skills in the least employable;
- expanding the role of independent providers in delivering employment services as widely as possible;
- allowing expert commercial and voluntary organisations a priority role in helping sick and disabled people into work;
- giving a bigger role to specialist charities in assisting 'hard-to-help' groups, such as the homeless, ex-offenders and drug users;
- helping parents by encouraging the expansion of affordable childcare.

By focusing on the problems that perpetuate inactivity and dependency, welfare reform can be the key to sustained high employment. Enabling the social market in welfare provision means driving business excellence into services and strengthening that activity with a social purpose. That purpose is never to write people off, but constantly to innovate to provide them with the best help towards achieving independence.

The Conservative Party has a strong tradition of social reform, personified by figures from as far back in history as Disraeli and Lord Shaftsbury. They made Britain a better place, and we must reaffirm their commitment. As we take forward our Party's vision for the future, we must let people know that we will confront, head on, the deprivation that blights their neighbourhoods and limits their chances.

I recognise that welfare reform is just one step towards a society in which everyone has the opportunity to achieve his or her best. We will also need to allow real meritocracy in education, so we can fully recognise the potential in every young person; we must help older people who have lost their jobs in traditional industries get the skills relevant to new ones, because everyone deserves a second chance; and we must drive discrimination out of the workplace, so no matter what your age, background or disability, you will always have the chance to prove your worth. The confidence we have in our values will help us forge a better Britain, united in its belief that everybody deserves the chance to fulfil their ambitions.

The consequences of state failure and the modern Conservative response

Rt Hon. David Davis MP

There was a time when the heart of the Conservative Party seemed to beat in time with the majority of British public opinion. Today, after three election defeats – and massive defeats at that – it is clear that something needs to change if we are ever to find that rhythm again. Almost every serious Conservative thinker now accepts this proposition. There are few who argue that 'one more heave' will be enough to see the Conservative Party returned to government.

The debate currently going on in the Party is therefore extremely welcome. But it is also in danger of appearing too introspective. Rather than asking 'what must we do to win', we should be asking 'what can we do for the country?'. The answer is that the Conservative Party alone can effect a fundamental change in British politics – a change that will open up opportunities for all those who feel trapped in the everyday frustrations of life in our country. By applying timeless Tory values of personal freedom and smaller government to the problems of today, we have an opportunity to reverse the growth of dependency and welfarism.

By promoting an agenda of empowerment – offering to put people in genuine control of their own lives – a modern Conservative Party can set out a distinctive programme for government, one that speaks to the hopes and aspirations of the British people. By changing the terms of the political settlement in Britain, we can give the victims of state failure, the people who have been most let down by New Labour, the opportunity to make the best of their lives.

Ronald Reagan once said that the nine most terrifying words in the English language are 'I'm from the Government and I'm here to help'. His comment reflected the age in which his presidency began. The 1980s saw governments in both Britain and America seeking to 'roll back' the reach of the state and to unleash the dynamism of individual people and businesses. The idealism of the time became so ingrained that even our political opponents now pay lip service to it. But as New Labour extends its reach into people's everyday lives, there is now a unique opportunity for us to make the case for a better balance between the roles of the state and of the citizen.

There are some things the state should do, like protecting the safety of the British people, but there is much that it currently tries to do which should rightfully be done by other means. Our task is to find the right balance between the two. The Conservative Party is well placed to do this because, unlike Labour, we recognise that poor government performance is at the root of so many of today's problems.

The patient queuing for treatment in hospital; the child leaving school unable to read or write; motorists struggling to get to work on congested roads – all are being failed by poor government. As a consequence of government encroachment into more and more areas of daily life, the number of people being failed by the system is growing. Worse still, many of these victims of state failure are already among the most disadvantaged people in our society. For example, unemployed people are twice as likely to be victims of violent crime; the poorest in society are the most likely to be burgled; people living on a council estate are twice as likely to have a vehicle stolen; the worst education and health outcomes are in the poorest areas; and the people most let down by poor government are also those least able to escape from it.

The better off have a reasonable chance of extricating themselves from the consequences of state failure. They can afford to protect and alarm their houses and to travel everywhere by car, they can opt-out of ever-lengthening waiting lists by paying to go private or using the private medical insurance that they get through employment, and they can afford to move to a more affluent area to get their children into a better school or they can opt to take them out of the state system altogether. But they are the fortunate few. Under New Labour, dependency is widespread and becoming locked in.

A third of households now rely on the state for more than half of their income, and the tax credits system is entrenching dependency and spreading it up the income scale. All of this damages hope and aspiration: people who are constantly told to know their place eventually learn not to expect anything better. As a result, Britain is becoming less socially mobile. Too many people feel trapped in situations beyond their control with little chance of escape, and they feel powerless in the face of a system that seems to have forgotten them. They have almost no control over vital areas of their lives, and almost no opportunity to improve their lot and to contribute to the wider health of our society. It is little wonder that British society is becoming increasingly fractious when opportunity and hope are so constrained.

Our communities are also plagued by rising levels of violent crime and by anti-social behaviour. Much of this is caused by young people with too little to do and too little to aspire to. They are unable to get on in schools that do not inspire them and fail to teach them the basics, and they know that they cannot get anywhere without a tertiary education, yet they cannot afford the time or the money to get one. Their frustration turns to crime. Lacking opportunities to better themselves, they end up caught in a spiral of decline which benefits no-one. How different could their lives have been if they had been given the chance of a better way?

The prevailing leftist orthodoxy suggests that the solution to these problems lie in special initiatives, new grants, state programmes, tsars, commissions, 'action zones', and all the rest of the paraphernalia that accompanies a quango state. It should be clear to all by now that this approach, tested to destruction by Labour over the past eight years, has not worked and will not work. We need a new approach and a better way.

The modern Conservative Party must be prepared to make the case for radical change. It is not enough to accept the terms of debate New Labour have set for us and to promise simply to make a few tweaks to their approach. We must seize the opportunity to set out an entirely new direction for public policy, a direction involving a new political settlement with a better balance in the relationship between politicians and the people. This settlement must be based on the acknowledgement that people know better than politicians do about how to improve their own lives. They just need to be given the chance.

Government's role is to remove the barriers to opportunity and to ensure, in Winston Churchill's memorable phrase, that there is 'a limit beneath which no man may fall but no limit to which any man might rise'. This is not just a call to roll back the frontiers of the state. It is much more than that. A modern Conservative Government must change the very way power is wielded in Britain: it must commit itself to a genuine transfer of power from the political elites to the people.

Gone are the days when people looked up to politicians – and the days when they were prepared to accept second best. As private consumers, people today are accustomed to receiving the particular service they demand when and where they demand it. In Britain's consumer society, people now know that they hold the cards. As consumers, they wield the power and, as a result, they get the best. A government that simply reverses some of Labour's more damaging policies while retaining as much power as possible in its own hands will not be able to satisfy the demands of a modern consumer society from its public services. Removing the barriers to opportunity is one half of the equation: giving people the power to make the most of those opportunities is the modern Conservative ideal.

The modern Conservative Party must be prepared to make the case for radical change. It is not enough to accept the terms of debate New Labour have set for us and to promise simply to make a few tweaks to their approach.

This is an argument that has been made very powerfully by some of the new generation of Conservative MPs. They have shown a willingness to embrace radical new ideas and to learn lessons from abroad that should give us hope that the Conservative Party can once again come to the aid of those who are being let down by the policies of a Labour Government.

In health and education, the changes we need are clear. Both services have been the subject of massive spending increases under Labour. Indeed, we now have amongst the most expensive public services in Europe. Yet they have not been transformed in the way Labour nor the British public might have expected in return. This is because both the health service and education system in Britain are run by central government, which acts as both funder and provider.

The notion that the state should be a monopoly supplier of services such as healthcare and education is part of an out-dated post-war consensus. There is no reason why we cannot hold true to the ideal of universal services while also making the case for a better way of providing them. Many other countries have grasped this point, and many of our near-neighbours in Europe have higher standards of healthcare and education as a result. In Germany, for example, 50% of hospitals are not owned by the state. Yet Germany's health system is superior to ours on almost every measure, including survival rates and the uptake of new medicines. In the Netherlands, 70% of schools are independently run, and their educational standards are generally excellent. It is from a British political perspective somewhat ironic that many countries in Continental Europe recognise the important role that the independent and voluntary sectors have to play when so many of them have governments from the left of centre.

These and other examples from abroad teach us that we can ensure every citizen has the chance of a good education and decent healthcare if we are prepared to end government monopolies and allow in the expertise and dynamism of the independent and voluntary sectors. Such an approach necessitates a fundamental shift in the balance of power between the state and the citizen, putting the state's spending power in the hands of patients, parents and other public service users. It would require the Government to let go and allow people to have more control over their own lives.

The modern Conservative Party must be willing to argue for the post-war consensus to be replaced with this new style of government fit for the 21st Century. In education, a system in which parents have real control will be more innovative and responsive to the needs of each individual child. Instead of having to fight the appeals panel process to get their children into good schools, parents will be courted by schools that want their children to be there. Schools will be writing to them, inviting them to visit, and promoting the benefits they have to offer. The balance of power will have moved from the education establishment to the parent – and the natural forces of competition will drive up standards across the board, giving more children the opportunity to go to a good school.

The modern Conservative aim to change centrally run structures that are not working to ones that put people in control also applies to healthcare, which is by its very nature personal. The NHS in its current form is the very embodiment of the old 'know-your-place' culture. Rigid, centralised policies mean that the bureaucracy holds all the cards, while patients have to stand in line until the system is ready to see them. The NHS should instead be a provider of personal healthcare, rather than national healthcare. Every patient should be treated based on their absolute need, not on their ability to pay or on the system's ability to deal with them. Once again, we need to shift the balance of power from the system to the individual. When all patients have the power to demand the treatment they want where they want it, standards will rise across the board as genuine accountability is introduced for the first time.

Transferring power from the state to the citizen is an agenda fit for the 21st century. In education and healthcare, the way to do this is clear. There are other areas, however, where the process requires a more tailored approach. It is obviously not possible to give individuals direct control of the police. Yet, again, experience abroad suggests that introducing real accountability delivers results. Conservatives have long pointed to New York as an example of successful policing. Yet Britain continues to take a very different approach, with the Home Secretary setting national targets and individual Chief Constables accountable to him and un-elected Police Authorities, rather than to the people they are supposed to serve.

While we cannot give people direct control of the police, we can empower them by allowing them to elect local police boards which would set the priorities and the direction for policing in local areas. Where we cannot empower people directly, we should empower communities instead. It is the job of central government to set a framework and to give individuals the opportunity to wield power within it.

There are some who argue that Britain is not ready for such a fundamental change in the relationship between the citizen and the state. They reason that the Conservative Party should focus more on standards rather than structures. Our challenge, though, is to make the case for change precisely because it will raise standards. We should not advocate it out of blind ideology, but because giving people greater control of their own lives is the way to achieve the outcomes we all want to see – the opportunity for everyone in Britain to receive the very best.

That must be our vision. A single nation in which everyone has the chance to get the best and to be the best. Such an outcome is not simply morally right; it is also the only way to begin to alleviate some of the many deep-seated problems in Britain today.

Democratic renewal, national identity and social justice: a modern agenda for government

John Tate

Britain and Britishness are political creations. As such, they need political impetus to survive. The British identity has long relied on fading understandings and conventions; to prosper it needs fresh articulation and action. The current government has made efforts in this area, but far deeper work remains.

The Conservative Party should, for reasons that I shall explain in this chapter, adopt a new agenda based on the concept and value of the democratic nation state. Not a backward looking agenda, but one of radical democratic reform – from parliamentary reform to a codified ('written') constitution. This new agenda should also mean making Britishness a more accessible identity, whether to disaffected Asian youths in Leeds or to the displaced people of Montserrat.

The Party's absence of leadership in this area has allowed New Labour to portray itself as the party of national identity. To justify this portrayal, the Prime Minister can point to the introduction of:

- citizenship classes – which the Conservative Party opposed;
- devolution for Scotland, helping quell demands for independence – which the Conservative Party opposed;
- fuller citizenship for Overseas Territory nationals – after the second-class citizenship foisted on them by a Conservative government in 1981;

- citizenship ceremonies for new British nationals.

These measures are far from perfect. A compelling, narrative account of British history would advance a child's sense of Britishness far more effectively than a citizenship class. Nonetheless, Labour can point to a package of measures that speak to what it means to be British. Given its patchy record in this area, which includes having made all Britons formal citizens of the European Union, the Conservative Party needs a compelling response.

The content of the British identity must of course be for the people at large to determine. My focus is on the value of and mechanisms for reinvigorating that identity. Overall, a new emphasis on Britishness, within a radical programme of democratic form, should promote greater social and territorial integrity.

i) The value of the nation-state in the face of univeralism

With important exceptions, Britons continue to believe in the democratic nation state as the final authority in matters of identity and law. Yet the nation state is under sustained attack, most significantly from different varieties of universalism. Whether in defence of human rights, free markets, world peace, or Marxism, universalist challenges to the nation state are based on the view that, for reasons practical and moral, nation states must no longer be the paramount constituencies in world affairs. As Denis Healey said of his intensely private Bilderberg group of leading international politicians, business people and journalists:

> To say we were striving for a one-world government is exaggerated, but not wholly unfair. Those of us in Bilderberg felt we couldn't go on forever fighting one another for nothing and killing people and rendering millions homeless. So we felt that a single community throughout the world would be a good thing.

The moral strand of most modern universalism lies in the notion of human rights – rights that necessarily transcend national jurisdictions. As President George W. Bush put it:

> We do share values. And, they're universal values, they're

not American values or, you know, European values, they're universal values. And those values, being universal, ought to be applied everywhere.

The practical strand of universalism is managerialism: the belief that capital, information, and population flows are now of such scale and speed that only supra- and international bodies can monitor, influence and accommodate them.

a) Moral universalism: human rights

The moral strand of universalism is based on the belief that too many right principles of human conduct transcend cultural and geographic boundaries for national sovereignty to be paramount. The essence of this position is evident when Westerners face illiberal treatment abroad. The universalist will object that facing the lash for theft, for example, is as wrong in the Gulf as it is in the West. They claim that certain rights transcend cultural grounds and are universal – the justification for them being, as the American Constitution has it, self-evident.

In *Spheres of Justice*, Professor Walzer provides a powerful objection to the universalist claim to transcend culture, arguing that justice depends on culturally relative understandings. Different goods – a title under which he includes intangibles like justice, education, and health – are, Walzer argues, understood in different societies to have different distribution principles. In one society the distribution of education may be understood to be properly based on academic merit; in another it may be based on means. Competing distribution principles – means, merit, need, *etcetera* – should in this way, he argues, be applied to different goods according to local understandings of those goods. To apply distribution principles – whether for education, health, or chocolate bars – without reference to local understandings is to create a less just and less authentic society.[20]

If the dominant understanding of healthcare in Britain is, as it appears to be, that it should be distributed according to the presence of illness, then medical need is that good's appropriate distribution principle. Accessing healthcare according to piety, financial wealth, or any other quality than illness, is to corrupt the sphere of justice that that good occupies.

There are important implications, on this view, for Conservative policy. The Party's promise to give citizens the 'right to choose' private healthcare – adding their own money to a state contribution – must be limited to gaining such things as better food or accommodation, and not better medical treatment, if the Party is to remain true to public understandings in Britain about the nature of healthcare.

Walzer's thesis is profound and raises a number of important questions that I do not have space to consider here. His central contention, however – that social justice depends on culturally relative understandings – is compelling.[21] In particular, it is vital that governance and law be grounded firmly in the societies in which they operate, within the framework of the democratic nation state. While seemingly uncontroversial, this grounding is becoming less and less secure.

Consider, for instance, the European Convention on Human Rights (ECHR). The Convention limits the ability of European nations to come to different conclusions on how the political tradeoffs inherent in rights should be resolved – from deciding what is defensible freedom of speech, for example, as opposed to incitement, or where the public's right to know impinges unacceptably on personal privacy. These intensely political tradeoffs are inherent in all rights, as illustrated in Article Ten of the Convention. Article Ten holds that:

> Everyone has the freedom of expression.

So far so unequivocal. Then come the politics, with a statement that this 'right' is:

> Subject to such formalities, conditions, restrictions or penalties as are prescribed by law and are necessary in a democratic society, in the interests of national sovereignty, territorial integrity or public safety, for the prevention of disorder or crime, for the protection of health or morals, for the protection of reputation or rights of others, for preventing the disclosure of information received in confidence, or for maintaining the authority and impartiality of the judiciary.

Like Article Ten, all so-called rights house multiple cross-pressures and potential contradictions. To put the resolution of these cross-pressures and contradictions beyond local communities, giving them instead to unaccountable (and, in the final instance, supranational) judges, is to neglect the cultural understandings that give justice meaning.

Universal human rights are nonsense precisely because rights conflict, the point of a judicial system being to arrive at fair proportion in the competing claims of citizens. Since the notion of fair proportion refers to things, the proportion sought by a judicial system must have boundaries. The search for proportion must obtain within a specific and well-defined social entity, a state, which is why statehood is the essential framework for law. Law also has an important social function: to maintain an ongoing order in which citizens can understand themselves and find meaning in their surroundings.

The Conservative Party should not be afraid to say that it does not believe in universal rights superior to democratic politics, provided that it explains why. Instead of merely reviewing the Act that incorporates the ECHR into UK law (the Human Rights Act, or HRA), as the Party promised to do in the run up to the last election, it should commit to withdrawing from the ECHR altogether as part of a package of democratic renewal. The Party's argument at the time – that it would consider scrapping the HRA due to a rise in the number of claimants citing Convention rights – was weak, since this was to be expected when the ECHR became actionable in UK courts and is not obviously worse than when, before the HRA, Conservative governments were repeatedly judged in breach by the European Court.

Instead of signing up to paper rights in Europe, we should demand that our elected representatives fulfil their duty to defend our liberties at home, in a sovereign Parliament. Under present arrangements, many will regard Parliament's ability to protect our liberties with scepticism – and, under present arrangements, they would be right to do so. This is why the Conservative Party must also commit to a radical programme of democratic reform, including parliamentary reform and a codified constitution (a subject to which I will return in the second part of this chapter).

b) Practical universalism: managerialism
The human rights strand of universalism dovetails with another

strand: managerialism. Here the argument is that capital, information, and population flows are now of such scale and speed that only supra- and international bodies can monitor, influence, and accommodate them. The accountability of these bodies is indirect and opaque.

There are at least two explanations for the democratic deficit surrounding managerialism. One is that the powers exercised by supranational authorities are apolitical. This apolitical/management principle is the basis of the significant power now exercised by supranational bodies like the International Criminal Court and the European courts; the European Central Bank and the World Bank; and the European Commission. Their governing principle is workmanship – the practical application of known principles, unfettered by democratic control. Yet, in fact, deciding whether to revalue a currency or prosecute a head of state is intensely political. Elevating these decisions to supranational banks and courts makes them no less political, only less accountable.

All issues must eventually leave the realm of accountable political decision-making, of course, and enter the realm of management and implementation; where precisely they do so is a difficult line to draw. Yet the trend toward drawing this line in favour of management and implementation is parasitic on democracy. As Dr John Laughland observes:

> Universalism leads to managerialism because it assumes that everyone's interests and goods are the same. This is the opposite of politics; the opposite of the assumption that people have intelligence and therefore different views on the world and society. Managerialism derives from a universalist and materialist view of mankind: the view that people are all driven by the same material desires rather than by the human need to live in an intelligible universe.

A second explanation for the democratic deficit surrounding managerialism is that its promoters consider that establishing direct, democratic control of supranational institutions is an unacceptable step toward world government. Many who criticise the EU for its democratic deficit are in this respect confused. Were supranational institutions like the EU made genuinely democratic, these critics would lack a defence of the genuine cause of their objection: their belief in the sovereign nation state. Opposition to supranationalism based on support for national sovereignty should not rely on arguments for democracy *per se*, therefore, but on arguments for the democratic nation state. Central to this alternative argument should be that social justice depends on a culturally bounded political community – the nation state.

c) The constituency problem

I have so far examined separate objections to the moral and practical strands of universalism. Another important objection applies to them both: what I shall call the constituency problem. This problem consists in the fact that the boundaries of a sovereign state cannot be created by majority vote. The EU, for example, may take a decision supported by the majority of its citizens. Britain may defect from the EU-wide decision, based on the support of a majority of its citizens. Citing a different majority view within its borders, Scotland may defect from the British decision, prompting still another defection of the Highlands of Scotland from the Lowlands. This defection problem could end with one-man constituencies. The point is clear: sovereign boundaries cannot sustainably be born of a majority vote.

Even one of the countries closest to direct democracy, the United States, has by constitutional design made it almost impossible for its component states to secede, with a blocking minority on constitutional change as low as 3% of its population. As President Lincoln argued when, forcibly and unconstitutionally, he re-united the United States: a country's boundaries must be fixed by some more primordial factor than the changing views of all of its component parts.[22]

The Conservative Party should recognise the truth of Lincoln's argument in relation to the post-imperial convention that areas under British sovereignty, from Overseas Territories to component states like Scotland, can gain independence by simple majority vote. No matter that majority opinions in these areas could change a year later; they would be independent, never to return. This 'biased finality' inherent in referendums, combined with the logic of integrated sovereignty articulated by Lincoln, should compel us to regard our sovereign boundaries as settled – without an automatic right for areas within them to secede. We should certainly not be equally willing to accept whatever position communities under British sovereignty wish to adopt, as the traditional Foreign Office view has it, any more than we should be happy to accept independence for Cornwall. We should strive for these communities – from Gibraltar to the Outer Hebrides; from disaffected Asian youths in Leeds to the displaced people of Montserrat – to actually want to remain British. Doing so would help confirm and develop our identity, while making it more accessible to others. Making the British identity accessible also means distilling it into easily learned and recognised narratives and symbols – whether a flag, a song, national celebrations, or a compelling version of national history taught in schools. Tacit understandings and conventions may be the more traditional British way, but the traditional way is failing. In this of all areas, the Conservative Party should lead the way.

A coherent account of the purpose and value of the democratic nation state would also help the Party to justify its position on the thorny question of immigration. Many commentators argue that immigration offers a solution to Britain's skills shortages. It was largely on this argument that *The Economist* headlined one of its commentaries on the subject 'Net immigration into Britain is higher than it has ever been – good'. For a variety of economic and demographic reasons, which need not detain us here, replacement migration is not, in fact, a satisfactory long-term solution to Britain's skill shortages. Yet some Conservatives are drawn to creating a free market in labour as the last great extension of international free trade. They should resist this attraction on the ground of what states are for. The free movement of labour is very different from the free movement of capital and goods. The relatively free movement of labour can produce great benefits, of course, as Anthony Browne observes:

> Allowing people to move from where their productivity is low to where their productivity is higher will raise the global output. It does this through increasing the livelihoods of immigrants themselves, and creating global centres of excellence such as the City of London,

Hollywood and Silicon Valley.

In Britain, the phenomenon Browne identifies is sometimes called the 'Wimbledon theory': provide a well-run venue open to the best international talent, and the results will benefit host and participants alike. Note, though, that the hosts Browne cites only offer access to an elite. Taken beyond an elite, to mass immigration, and the practice flounders on the notion of what human communities are for, and why migration between them is fundamentally different from flows of capital and goods. Nations rightly have stricter entry criteria for people than they do for capital and goods, as those criteria are part of what make them nations.

ii) The case for radical democratic renewal

The new emphasis on nationhood I have discussed in this chapter should be advanced through a radical programme of democratic renewal. This renewal should begin with constitutional reform and extend to the reform of Parliament, local government, and the Conservative Party itself.

Conservatives have traditionally prized the organic nature of our constitution for its flexibility. The conventions that underpin this flexibility, however, have been stretched and broken beyond repair. The so-called right of residual freedoms – by which Britons are free to do anything not prohibited in law – is often compared favourably with the situation in many continental European countries – where the law often defines what can be done. The problem is that as the Statute Book has grown our residual freedoms have shrunk. Our residual freedoms, like our constitution, have been constricted between an activist European Commission legislating on everything from horse manure to employment rights, and a succession of activist governments in Westminster proposing ever more legislation to fill 'gaps' in the law. The filling of these 'gaps' – our residual freedoms – has turned our law from a string vest into chain mail. Market traders are tried for weighing goods in pounds and ounces. Teachers are barred from teaching if they do not pay fees to a newly compulsory quango, the General Teaching Council. Horse owners must buy passports for their animals.

Politically, electorally, constitutionally, the UK has become a mixed-up and misshapen entity. The upper house of Parliament lies in limbo between a feudal past, a patronage-based present, and an uncertain democratic future. Areas under British sovereignty – from the Channel Islands, to the Overseas Territories, to Scotland, Northern Ireland and Wales – have more than six different constitutional relationships with Westminster. Parliament is notionally sovereign, but has long-since been overridden externally by EU law and, internally, by the near-total dominance of the executive and political parties.

In response to these developments, and as the central plank of a democratic renewal agenda, the Conservative Party should propose a codified constitution, enshrining the essential procedural principles of our government. Uppermost in this document should be explicit affirmation of the sovereignty exercised on behalf of the monarch by the people's representatives in Parliament. This affirmation would require amendments to the European Communities Act 1972 making clear that Parliament's sovereignty applies notwithstanding Britain's membership of the EU.[23]

The House of Lords, having been stripped of the only justification for its feudal organisation (the fact that it worked), should be made, like most other upper chambers in the Western world, democratically elected – albeit on different cycles and for different duties than Members of the House of Commons. The current position of many in the Conservative Party – that the upper chamber should be 'largely elected' – is mistaken, for it implies that democracy is not the only legitimate basis on which to select members of the nation's legislature. The prevailing view of the British public, I contend, is that

23 These amendments would be along the lines those proposed by Bill MP in his Sovereignty Parliament Bill (2004)

The argument that an elected upper chamber would challenge the Commons' supremacy begs an obvious question: why should the Commons be supreme?

democracy is in fact the only legitimate principle in this exercise – that lawmakers must be accountable through the ballot box for the laws that they make.

The argument that an elected upper chamber would challenge the Commons' supremacy begs an obvious question: why should the Commons be supreme? We are told that two elected chambers may produce legislative gridlock, yet this point is weak. Experience abroad shows that functional and procedural demarcations allow legislatures to accommodate split party control and avoid gridlock. Authoritative studies of the United States Congress show periods of split party control (where different parties control the House of Representatives and the Senate) to be quite productive. And even if ending the supremacy of the Commons did lead to legislative gridlock, it is not at all clear that less legislation would be a particularly bad thing in this country.

A democratic reform agenda should also mean liberating the Commons from overweening control by the executive and by political parties. MPs should have more free (un-whipped) votes and parliamentary committees more independence. Another powerful remedy would be to return to the Commons control over of its own standing orders.

Direct democracy should also be part of this reform agenda, allowing the British people to take control of their communities through locally elected offices such as that of sheriff, as well as other measures discussed in greater detail by Douglas Carswell. Instead of making matters of conscience the subject of free votes in Parliament, they could be decided in national referendums (after all, we do not on the whole regard our MPs as representing us on matters of conscience). To lessen the biased finality of referendums, mentioned above, the procedure could be triggered and re-triggered by parliamentary vote or by the collection of a given number of signatures. Signature campaigns could also be used to force a sitting member of Parliament to face his or her constituency for re-election.

A democratic reform agenda would further require the Conservative Party to lead by example in matters of its own organisation. The leader of the Party should certainly not be able summarily to prevent an MP from standing for re-election. Wider reform in this area could include open primaries, with Conservative parliamentary candidates selected in meetings open to any registered voter. An obvious danger of this method is that other parties may interfere with such meetings, though it is worth noting that open primaries in the United States are remarkably free of this (the dangers are small provided that the meeting agenda and candidates offered for selection remain under the Party's control). The potential benefits of the system are considerable – such that an open primary could even constitute one round of the contest to become the Conservative Party's leader. Benefits of open primaries include:

- an important new source of political education and civic; participation, in a country where citizens are usually unaware even of the identity of their parliamentary representative
- a radical 'trust the people' message;
- a potential boost to Party membership;
- more media coverage, helping catapult even relatively unknown candidates into the limelight and thereby create a wider pool of 'known faces' within the Party.

I have mentioned only a few of the measures that might form part of a democratic renewal agenda for the Conservative Party; there are many more. The important thing is that the Party occupy this terrain with credible and ambitious proposals, going far beyond reactive policies like 'English votes for English laws' (preventing Scottish MPs voting on matters that exclusively affect England and Wales); a 'largely elected' upper chamber; and 'reviewing' the Human Rights Act.

The Conservative Party should become champions of a more democratic, more transparent constitutional settlement. In rejecting universalism and declaring its faith in the democratic nation state, the Party would enhance the wellspring of law and social justice, and promote Britain's social and territorial integrity.

Conservative visions

Rt Hon. John Redwood MP

The European Social Model

The best social model, said Nicolas Sarkozy, is one that gives people a job. Well functioning market economies allow all to find a role and join in the quest for prosperity. In that sense, Europe's Social Model is positively anti-social: it is failing the jobless and must be abandoned.

The problem with the European social model is that it is based on several false assumptions. For example, European theorists and bureaucrats believe that the European economy can be protected from the competitive tax regimes of Asia and the Americas, meaning that we can have a social conscience about poverty in Africa and Asia, but that we should never open our own markets to overseas products sufficiently to help solve the problem.

European theorists also believe that more European integration creates greater solidarity between the member states, leading to greater social justice. They ignore the conflicts and disagreements between countries that the Brussels 'one size fits all' policies foment. This approach is motivated by those in the EU government who think no member state's economy should be allowed to prosper more rapidly than the average, but rather all should be brought down to the lowest common denominator through more intervention, more government and more regulation. Lower taxes are viewed as 'unfair tax competition' and less regulation as 'regulatory dumping'. This will only serve to hobble the EU economy, and then shut it off from the rest of the world, lest we notice how far behind we are falling.

The results of all Europe's legislative and governmental efforts have been worrying. European growth year after year falls well short of the United States of America. As China opens up individual industries to overseas capital investment and entrepreneurship, so Europe discovers that jobs go eastward and its own industries falter. Europeans have little answer to the Chinese success at making colour televisions and DVDs and are now seeing the strength of China's manufacture of textiles and leather products. Although one in ten people of working age are unemployed on a regular basis in the principal continental countries, the European Union concentrates more and more effort on protecting the jobs of those who are lucky enough still to have them, drawing a veil over those who cannot find one.

In the United Kingdom, we can offer people something so much better. Where the European Union offers introspection, we should offer wider horizons. Where it offers more regulation and government, we should offer more freedom. Where it seeks to protect Europe from the strong competitive forces of the Americas and Asia, we should welcome them and work alongside them. Where the European Union is happy to have higher levels of unemployment, we should promote enterprise and job creation. Where the European Union wants to control its citizens by more and more laws, we should make them freer by cutting the Statute Book and giving more responsibility to individuals.

Conservatism – a belief in aspiration, hope and freedom

The Conservative Party needs to be a party of aspiration, hope and freedom. We should be angry that social mobility has been in decline for nearly a decade. We should campaign restlessly against sink schools and sink estates where people have been made prisoner by public provision, and where a Tax Credit culture has placed the highest effective tax rates on those who can least afford them at the lower end of the income scale. We should object strongly to the taxes that have been imposed on those who save for their pension and those who seek to buy their own home. Under a Labour government, the average age for buying a first home is now 34,[24] meaning a whole generation of twenty-somethings are living at home with parents or in rented accommodation, often against their wishes. The best pension provision in Western Europe has been wrecked

24 First-time buyers older', *The Guardian*, 2005.

through penal taxation and an attack on company profits.

Wider ownership

The Conservative Party should be the party of wider ownership. We made rapid strides in the 20th century, spreading home ownership ever more widely, and transforming a country of tenants into a country of homeowners. The attractive policy of selling council housing to those who rented it was bitterly contested by Labour but was triumphantly successful, with Labour Councillors finding it so attractive that even they bought their own homes. They were right to do so.

A new Conservative government must ignite the torch of ownership once again by selling off housing association and council property on favourable terms to those who otherwise could not afford to own their own homes, and also by increasing the amount of affordable housing for sale and promoting shared ownership schemes to bridge the gap for those on low incomes. People are happier and have more opportunity in life if they own a stake in their society – they enjoy a pride of ownership and a freedom to decide what to do with their homes, how to decorate them, whether to extend them, how to use them. Owned homes are maintained to higher standards than public rented accommodation, and people are encouraged to take an interest in local and national politics to try to prevent politicians from damaging the security of their homes.

A Conservative government should also promote wider ownership of industry and commerce. The large privatisation programmes of the 1980s created a new generation of shareholders far larger than any preceding one, and it was discovered that giving employees free shares was an effective way to motivate them: when people come to own a share in the company they work for, they gain a pride in that company and approach their tasks in a different spirit. When the lorry drivers of National Freight acquired shares in that former nationalised enterprise, there was a revolution in the way they thought. One lorry driver explained, 'when I worked for a state concern and the lorry didn't work, I gave it a kick and then said I could not take it out that day. Now I own a share of the lorry it's different. I give it a polish and make sure it works'. When did you last see someone washing a rented car? That is why the

Conservatives must make selling the Post Office to its employees part of a new programme to spread share ownership ever more widely.

We also need to stimulate more enterprise in small businesses and the self-employed. One of the successes of recent decades has been a large increase in the numbers of those who work for themselves. Yet under this Government, it has become very difficult to become self-employed, with more and more demands and requirements placed upon those who work in their own company. We need to cut away a lot of the regulation that impedes and deters those entrepreneurs who want to set up small businesses, and create an even more favourable tax system for them.

Make every school an independent school

A Conservative government needs to tackle the problem of poor schools. It is well known that in our inner city areas too many schools fail their pupils. Teachers in those areas are well aware of the problems of trying to teach young people who have no serious interest in education because they have no belief that it will help them in their future lives. Yet the problem is no longer limited to the inner cities or the poorest districts: there are many state schools in suburbs and shires with mediocre results, and too many parents still think it is worthwhile making the heroic sacrifice of paying for a private school education for their children they can scarcely afford because they want an education that can produce better results and more confidence in their children.

This has led us to a Britain where parents can buy real advantage by sending their children to a fee-paying school if they have the money, but are debarred if they do not. It is high time that all schools enjoyed independent status, so that governing bodies and head teachers can be given the freedoms that independent schools already have. In addition, the state should pay to send pupils to a school of their choice (whether state or fee-paying) up to fixed maximum fee each year, with parents free to top-up the state fee if they wish. Scholarship money should also be made available so that those from the poorest backgrounds would have the opportunity to go to any school in the country whatever the fee level. This would ensure that the state could both guarantee a better quality school than is currently available by providing a fixed fee for everyone who wanted it and ensure that people from low-income backgrounds had an equal opportunity to those from high-income backgrounds to access the dearest schools. Let all have a chance to go to Eton – let those who do best at the exams win the state scholarships available to go.

This would be an effective method to improve standards because it would make parents and students powerful in deciding which school to go to and therefore how the school should perform. Bad schools would be forced to change, otherwise they would attract insufficient pupils. Good schools would have the extra money needed to expand as they attracted more to come. Quality would spread through the schooling system just as surely as good ideas spread through all the competitive market places serving most other customer needs. At the same time as schools were made independent, we could make huge savings in cutting out the local education authority bureaucracy and removing the regulations on schools from central government. There would be no need for a national curriculum or for government ministers to opine on how schools should teach: independent schools would be more likely to choose difficult exams for good pupils to sit, to help universities select the best.

Similarly, universities should be made more independent, allowing university professors to do more outside the university to bring the university closer to the worlds of business and professional life. The tax regime should be made more generous for universities to build up their independent endowments.

Scholarship money should also be made available so that those from the poorest backgrounds would have the opportunity to go to any school in the country whatever the fee level.

The state should earmark the proceeds of some asset sales from the government to build up their endowments at the beginning of the process.

Free health care in the surgery or hospital of your choice
We need a similar reform of the Health Service. What people value about the Health Service is the promise of care free at the point of use when they need it, but they despair of the inability of the public sector to fulfil this pledge despite huge sums of extra money having been routed into the Health Service year after year. When people get the free treatment in the hospital they are usually grateful for it. They are not grateful if they are told that they need surgery but they may have to wait six months or a year to get it. They are even less grateful if they contract a serious infection in hospital when their turn finally comes for treatment.

Yet people are not hung up on who owns and runs their hospitals and surgeries: we have a hybrid system in any case, as GPs are largely independent contractors, now carrying out more and more work in the private sector. Surgeons in NHS hospitals also often have private practices in smaller hospitals for BUPA and PPP. Thus, the nationalisation of hospital buildings and many of the other staff, which took place after the war, is not necessarily the right model to follow in the 21st century: large, heavily unionised hospitals do not seem to be delivering the quality of care in a timely way that the public wants and expects. We need to offer people more choice and more power over the care they require.

We should honour the pledge that all who need it get the care they require free at the point of use. We should allow private hospitals and private surgeries to flourish alongside the state-owned ones and let people choose.

In health as in education, we need far more freedom and far less regulation. We should honour the pledge that all who need it get the care they require free at the point of use. We should allow private hospitals and private surgeries to flourish alongside the state-owned ones and let people choose. Public money should follow the choices people make. We should also allow top-up payments for people who wish to see a private sector doctor or hospital where the fees are higher than the nationally agreed maximum for NHS patients.

Flatter and lower tax rates are good for the government as well as for everyone else
An enterprise economy requires lower taxes. The United Kingdom took a great leap forward when in the 1980s we slashed the top rate of tax on so-called unearned income from 98% to 40% and the rate of tax on earned income from 83% to 40%. We also cut the standard rate of tax to only 23%. This gave Britain a great relative advantage and started the renaissance of the British economy. Today, the successful and enterprising parts of the world have more than caught up. Many have now overtaken us. Tax rates of 40% and 22% today are not competitive by the best standards worldwide. Worse still are the rates of up to 70% that British people are paying when they combine the marginal tax rate with the rate of withdrawal of Tax Credit or benefit. This acts as a great disincentive to do better, and the complexities of such a system also lead to many mistakes by both the government and the taxpayer.

The United States of America has shown that by cutting taxes under George W. Bush the economy benefits greatly. As with Reagan, so with Bush: the cut in tax rates after a period even leads to a lowering of the government deficit, as there is a surge in tax receipts resulting from the reduced rates and the improved performance of the economy. The Irish economy has responded magnificently to very low rates of corporate tax. Ireland has offered complete tax breaks for a period for new investors followed by a rate of 10% on corporate profits, leading to a significant increase in the number of businesses moving to Ireland to invest and in the number of Irish people returning to their home country to enjoy the better job prospects.

The United Kingdom should aim to cut its income and company tax income rates in order to promote greater prosperity and enterprise. We should cut income tax to 20% and company profits' tax to 20%. We should extend the 10% band upwards in the income scale and reduce the top rate from 40% to 30%. We should also abolish Capital Gains Tax on all assets held for more than two years and tax as income all gains realised in less than two years. This would once again place Britain amongst the leaders in the world economy, offering a more sensible tax regime for foot-loose investors and savers worldwide, and would attract many more successful companies and entrepreneurs, spending their money with us and being taxed here. It would also boost public spending and public services, because it would boost the economy. Above all, it would give a boost to those on the lower incomes currently caught in the tax-benefit trap, and make more jobs available to help them.

Everyone agrees we need to deregulate – so let's get on with it
An incoming Conservative government must above all set people free. Four thousand new laws have been created every year over the last decade. This government has become too enthusiastic in this approach, believing there is a regulatory answer to every problem, and in some cases creating new problems in order to justify regulation. Yet our experience of this has been predictably disappointing: in some cases, regulations achieve the opposite of what they set out to achieve. In others, regulations achieve nothing, and in yet others the modest gains they might make are offset by the very high costs and difficulties they impose.

Let us take the case of financial service regulation. Reacting to certain scandals in the past, the Government has greatly strengthened the amount of supervisory work carried out through the Financial Services Authority. The FSA proceeds by imposing substantial compliance costs on businesses that are largely or wholly compliant. This deters them from doing more business in Britain, encouraging them to look elsewhere for a less regulated place. It also deters innovation, as it is extremely difficult to fight through a new product or new idea to gain the necessary regulatory approvals.

On the other hand, it does not prevent the crooked continuing to break the law and do damage. If someone is thinking of defrauding savers and investors, breaking the law of theft, they are unlikely to be deterred by the fact that they will also have to commit the lesser crime of misleading the regulator. People want regulators to act as super cops, intercepting criminal activity in financial services before it damages them. Yet the regulators themselves seem to define their job as controlling the lives of those who work in the financial services industry and making it more difficult for them to operate in an enterprising spirit. Far from serving the customer better, the advent of comprehensive FSA regulation has increased the costs and charges savers have to pay, and has also pushed quite a lot of business offshore.

Take another example: speed cameras. Speed cameras were billed as the way to improve road safety and cut the number of traffic-accident related deaths. There was, of course, a consensus supporting this objective. However, as the Government has come to rely more and more upon speed control through speed cameras, we have witnessed a reversal in the trend to fewer and fewer fatal and dangerous accidents. After years of success through encouraging good driving and through sensible policing, we are now at a point where, for several years, there has been a rising trend in the number of fatal and serious injuries on the roads. The reason for this is simple: speed was not the main or primary cause of most accidents. Most accidents occur within the speed limit at junctions where there is more scope for the conflict between different types of road user travelling in different directions to cause an accident.

Because the government has switched its safety policy to speed control and speed cameras, there are now fewer police watching out for bad and dangerous driving at junctions, and so accidents have increased. Similarly, the reduction of traditional policing on our roads has allowed far more people to drive without licences, without insurance, and in stolen vehicles. This group of people are much more likely to be involved in dangerous accidents than law-abiding motorists who have tax, insurance, and are driving their own vehicle. Speed cameras cannot tackle this problem. The solution to safety problems on the road is better driving and different attitudes by drivers, combined with better junction and road design. Instead, under this government, highway authorities have been encouraged to make road design more dangerous and worse in many cases through the advent of chicanes, humps, road narrowing and lane closures. The government has also diverted the police into regarding speed as the only problem on the roads to the detriment of sensible policing of the things more likely to cause accidents. We need to deregulate and return to common sense enforcement of a requirement for people to drive sensibly in relation to the local conditions.

One of the best recent examples of unnecessary regulation is the combined effort of the European Union and the British government to over-regulate herbal remedies and food supplements. Many people in Britain are convinced that vitamin supplements, for example, help them to lead healthy lives. However, regulators are now demanding that all such food supplements be treated as if they were pharmaceuticals and put through expensive and exhaustive tests and clinical trials. The result is that many of the smaller producers will be unable to meet the cost and will close, and many retailers will face difficulties as the price of those products that remain on the shelves will rise, deterring their clientele.

The UK would be much better off without this unnecessary regulation of perfectly safe natural products. There can continue to be a debate between the medical professions who claim that these products achieve little or nothing, and the herbalists who believe that they are very successful in treating certain conditions. I am in favour of openness concerning the claims of these products and the requirement that their bottles should be properly labelled. Yet I see no need to go a step further and effectively drive some of these products out of the market altogether in the name of safety, when there is absolutely no evidence that these products have been unsafe or caused untimely deaths in the past. This is a case of regulation being a sledgehammer to miss the nut.

There is also far too much regulation of the labour market. The Working Time Directive, for example, was introduced with a view to limiting the number of hours people had to work. It offered the prospect of more leisure time and time with the family to those who had been working long hours. Yet it is also extremely damaging to the economy's ability to generate jobs, and a big incursion on personal freedom. It might as well be renamed the 'Abolition of Overtime' Directive. Many people want the flexibility and freedom to work more than 48 hours a week if they are seeking to save for their deposit for their first home, or put something away in the run-up to Christmas. This Directive prevents them from doing so for their principal employer; however, it does not prevent people from working longer hours if they wish. What we now have to do is acquire a second job with a different employer to work the extra hours. A long distance lorry driver who used to be able to work a 60 hour week instead of 48 hours because he wanted the overtime will now have to get a job, perhaps at a lower hourly rate of pay at the weekend, in order to make up the family earnings. It does not improve his quality of life or protect him in any way; it simply obstructs a sensible answer to his requirements.

This example is one part of the process by which the European Union is giving the economic advantage to less regulated places abroad. A British trucking company enforcing the 48 hour working week will have to charge its customers more, as it will need to incur the extra costs of recruiting new people and training them to do the additional driving the existing pool of drivers used to be able to achieve through overtime. Some of the clients of these businesses might decide it would be better to give their contract to a company based outside the European Union that does not have to comply with such rules. This is also another reason why British products and services may be less competitive than their Chinese counterparts, as the former's transport costs have recently been increased by European regulation.

If problems are global, so are solutions
A lot of the environmental regulation carried out nationally or on a European scale can be equally self-defeating. We all wish to clean up the planet, but we must understand that to do so we need global, not just European, agreement. There is little point in us imposing such stringent environmental controls on British businesses that they decide to shift their work to China or India, countries manufacturing in a much dirtier way than

we do here in Western Europe. There is a huge transfer of business activity under way from the European Union to China and India in any case, as a result of high taxes and high regulatory costs. Any additional increment in regulatory protection is going to tip more business in that direction. China is currently meeting her voracious demands for energy by building more coal-burning power stations. The coal China has in abundance is high in sulphur, which means much more dirty energy being produced.

It should be the Conservative message that technology is the answer to problems like environmental degradation and undesirable work. Mechanisation can take out of a factory the drudge jobs, the dirty and dangerous jobs, and give them to a machine. The exciting new technologies and markets for methane and carbon sinks emerging from the United States are more likely to solve the global environmental problem than the regulations being set by the EU. A positive Conservative message should be that we can be green, clean and prosperous.

I often hear people claim that unless we make richer countries and richer people poorer, the future is bleak. Yet travelling the world, the conclusion I reach is that the world would be a cleaner, better, finer place if we made the poor rich, rather than the rich poor. You cannot make the poor rich by making the rich poor, but you can make the poor rich by encouraging the rich to be outward-going with the wealth and power that they currently enjoy. If you create the right conditions then the rich will want to invest, open factories, and create jobs in the poorest parts of the world. If you create the right conditions where the rich can enjoy the comforts of lifestyle that motivated them to become rich in the first place, then you are more likely to harness their energies to solve the problems of poverty, environmental degradation and injustice that abound in the world.

All monopolies conspire against their users
My constituents do not come to me saying that they have problems getting the food they want or that there is not enough of it. There is no shortage of hotel bedrooms in Britain, and we do not have to queue for six months before gaining access to a hotel bed in the town of our choice. There is no difficulty in getting CDs, colour televisions or cars. Extremely sophisticated

pieces of equipment are available at affordable prices with a huge choice for the customer. The offers in the shops and showrooms are backed up by a plentiful supply of credit for those who wish to buy them before they have saved enough to pay.

The services and products that cause my constituents the most difficulties are all provided by the public sector. For example, there is a shortage of places at good schools. Every summer there is a scramble in my constituency and elsewhere in the country as parents desperately try to get their children in to the one or two schools that do really well and avoid a mandatory place at one of the others. There are endless problems for people trying to get the health care that they need when they want it. Our hospital system is short of beds, so a patient may have to wait six months before one is allocated to him. Whilst it is easy buying a car, it is far more difficult using it because of the shortage of road space supplied by the monopoly highways provider. The public is regularly told that they are greedy and selfish to want to travel by car and that they should instead switch to the train. Yet those who do discover there is a similar shortage of train capacity at peak times on popular routes, again the result of public sector control of the infrastructure.

It is good that the Labour government have accepted the case the Conservatives made when in office that the state is not the best means of delivering phone services, gas or electricity supply, or even water. Yet it is a step backwards that they now believe that they can have all the benefits of nationalisation (whatever they think they might be) by the back door through regulation which seeks to influence or control what private sector companies do in a competitive market. Government intervention and action can prevent competitive forces doing a better job in important service areas. The government has refused to allow full competition in water, meaning we have less water at a higher price than if they did allow competing providers to enter the system and provide the service. Above all, the government perseveres with monopoly district general hospitals and in some places monopoly comprehensive schools.

The world will work better if we empower people and control government

A Conservative government should offer something very different. We should tell people that if we wish to catch up with American living standards, and if we wish to compete with China and India in the global economy, then we need to change the way we do things. We need to opt for the low tax, lightly regulated option. This means, among other things, breaking the remaining public sector monopolies and reassuring people that under a Conservative government they will continue to enjoy the promise of free care at the point of use and a free school place for all those who need it. We can achieve this by freeing up the provision of both health and schooling to deliver more to a higher standard and in a more timely way than the failed public monopoly model has managed to do. More government is not the answer – it is often the problem.

The British economy has been relatively strong compared with our European neighbours, as a result of the lower taxes and labour market reforms carried out in the 1980s. We are now using up our historical capital rapidly and failing to understand just how rapidly others in the world are going well beyond what we then achieved. We need a dramatic change of direction. We need to tell our partners that we are not going to be drawn into the European social model or the integrated super state inherent in the constitution. We are happy to trade with them and be friends with them, but we wish to be outward looking and to recognise that our future lies with America and Asia much more than with ailing Europe.

A Conservative government should offer better education to those trapped in the inner cities, lower taxes to those setting out establishing their own businesses, less regulation to those already running established businesses, and greater freedom to all our citizens. We should be the party of economic growth, of modern technology, of greater prosperity. To do so we need to encourage choice and competition. The one business in Britain that we need to make less productive is the law making business.

We have more government than we need, more government than we want, and more government than we can afford. We must trust people more, and trust government less. That way we can give more people a sense they belong. We can create a fairer society, based on opportunity for all and ownership for the many.

Europe beyond Lisbon

Dr Liam Fox MP

Europe is at a crossroads. This has been said many times before and, on most occasions, it has been an exaggeration. Not on this occasion, however.

Superficially, the only triggers for this situation were the no votes in the French and Dutch referendums on the European Constitution. That is to over-simplify matters, however. The wider question for Europe is not how Member States should be governed by Brussels – much less, as it happens – but how they can rise to the economic challenges posed by China, India and the Americas. Europe's only answer to this question to date has been the Lisbon Agenda. That will not be enough.

It falls to the Conservative Party to make the rest of Europe realise that they need to adopt the programme of economic reforms which the UK carried out under the Thatcher Governments in the 1980s.

Guy Verhofstadt, the Prime Minister of Belgium, said in 2004 that:

> Growth in Europe last year was 0.8%, in the United States it was over 3%, in China it was over 10% [...] If we don't change things, we risk turning Europe into a social and economic museum.

It would not be hard to find exhibits for Mr Verhofstadt's museum. The present reality for 'social Europe' is grim. Unemployment in France has hovered between 8 and 10% for over twenty years, and shows no sign of a downward trend. France's new Prime Minister has explicitly rejected supply-side reforms of any significance.

In Germany, over five million are unemployed, with the rate running at 20% in the old east. DaimlerChrysler, Volkswagen, Deutsche Bank, Karstadt and many other major employers have been cutting thousands of jobs. According to *The Economist*, last year 'the top 24 industrial companies in Germany reduced their investment in Germany by 20% and worldwide by 10%'.[25]

This 'European Museum' comes with high costs – economic and social. It costs more to hire people, as well as to make them redundant, in 'social Europe' than here in the UK. The welfare bill is huge, and so personal taxation tends to be higher. Neither characteristic encourages entrepreneurial activity. Unemployment in Germany is 11.8% and in France it is 10.2%. In Britain, on the other hand, the rate is only 4.7%.

This makes it all the more bizarre that the Labour Government in Britain is gradually adopting much of the French and German Social Model, and in the process silting up our own economy in the same way that the French and Germans have done over the last three decades. Gordon Brown's preferred weapon for responding to economic downturns is to rely on consumer spending, which is both reckless and incompetent.

All this is not to say that the situation is all bleak, even in old Europe. There are success stories. Substantial investment is turning Dresden once more into the 'Florence of the Elbe', as glorious structures like the Frauenkirche are rebuilt after wartime devastation. But for every Dresden, there are many smaller towns and cities in the old East Germany where populations have plummeted by up to a third since reunification as the working population has fled west. Left behind are the old and economically inactive, creating communities that are socially unsustainable.

In the accession countries, on the other hand, there are many examples of economic dynamism. Adaptive, pioneering economies are leaping ahead. Estonia is just one accession state which is pioneering a flat tax, for example. Slovakia has become a European Detroit, as the leading centre of automotive production in the EU.

More and more EU Member States recognise that jobs and prosperity flow from a flexible labour market and a light-touch

25 *The Economist*, 7 2005.

approach to regulation. Those countries know that free trade and competition offer the best routes to sustained economic growth. Estonia is predicting 6% GDP growth this year and Slovakia 4%. These nations have no wish to be stifled by the centralising, regulatory tendencies of Brussels; no craving for the French and German Social Model. The Anglo-Saxon model of economic liberalism is the one to which they are attracted.

The only surprise about this is that anybody finds it surprising. The governments of the new democracies of east and central Europe have seen, like the rest of us, what has happened to the French and German economies as a result of heavy social costs. Their own economies had clogged up under Communism. Why would they perpetuate their own sclerosis? They wanted, naturally, to move in the opposite direction and encourage entrepreneurial activity.

By the turn of the century, there was finally a dawning realisation in some parts of Europe that the only way to transform the ailing Social Model economies was to adopt the supply-side reforms pioneered in 1980s Britain by the Conservative Party. The result was the Lisbon Agenda, launched in 2000. The goal of the Agenda, in brief, was to ensure that, by 2010, the nations of the European Union would constitute 'the most competitive and dynamic knowledge-based economy in the world'. Increasing employment levels was a core aim, to be achieved by removing the obstacles to employing the low-paid. The Agenda provided for higher and better IT usage as well as research and development. Targets on the environment were also included.

On paper, the Agenda was laudable. Sadly, it has barely had any impact, since it has largely remained on paper, rather than being translated into meaningful action. The EU still has twenty million unemployed. Net job creation has actually slowed down. Little progress has been made on the IT side. The environmental targets, while worthwhile, were not entirely germane to the wider goal of economic growth and job creation.

The failure of the Lisbon Agenda – and, sadly, it is not too early to pronounce it a failure – is little short of disastrous for Europe. The twenty million unemployed people within the European Union's borders represent not just a waste of human talent and enterprise but also a real threat to financial stability, making welfare systems increasingly difficult to sustain.

Unfortunately, many European leaders continue to delude themselves. They have a Eurocentric view of the world. They look at a map and see Europe in the middle and think that means that they must be in the middle of the global market.

It is no coincidence that, over recent years, many more jobs have been created in the United States than in the EU, or that the United States has actually been increasing its share of world trade. Social democratic policies are making Europe less competitive in an ever-more competitive global economic environment.

On a rapidly ageing continent, the omens do not look good. By 2010, the EU's working age population will have begun a seemingly permanent decline. Over the next 40 years, the working age populations of Germany, Italy and Spain will all fall by a third.[26] This will have a major impact on the European economy. The EU's own projections suggest that economic growth in Europe will be only half of that of America between now and 2050. Projected forward, the EU's share of global Gross Domestic Product will slump from 18% now to just 10% by the middle of the century, while America's share rises from 23 to 26%.[27]

Many thought and hoped that the EU would have regarded this gloomy picture as a timely wake-up call. Instead, the principles of Lisbon have been allowed to gather dust. The actual Agenda, meanwhile, has been allowed to grow too long. In 2004, the IMF calculated there were 102 separate Lisbon benchmarks, progress on which was, and is, slow. The OECD's Economic Survey of the Euro Area in 2004 said: 'structural reforms required to move the euro area economy towards the ambitious targets set by the Lisbon summit, have been hesitant and piecemeal'.

An internal EU review by former Dutch Prime Minister Wim Kok, published in November 2004, was equally critical. It suggested that Lisbon risked 'becoming a synonym for missed objectives and failed promises'.

The wider truth is that Lisbon is doomed to fail in the current 'version' of Europe. The European Union is a bureaucracy, consumed by a rationale to act and to intervene. The EU can certainly load on social costs, which damage the competitive-

26 Christopher Smal chief economic advise Barclays Bank, June 2

27 Dr Liam Fox MP, S to the Heritage Found Washington D.C. *The European Union - Wh Now?*, 22 June 2005

ness of European economies, but there is little it can do actually to enhance a national economy's effectiveness. That can be done only by individual nations. Too few observers have grasped this fundamental reality. Existing problems are being exacerbated by the willingness of too many European leaders to blame someone else for their economic woes. There is no point in either the French or German Governments blaming external factors for the dreadful performance of their economies. Unless leaders in France and Germany have the courage and commitment to introduce supply-side reforms, then they will consign yet another generation of their young people to structural unemployment. This cannot be an acceptable price to pay to keep the political classes inside their comfort zone.

The obvious remedy is the adoption of the market-orientated economic changes undertaken by the UK and the US in the 1980s. There is no need to spell them out chapter and verse here; the model is tried and tested, and has been written about exhaustively. Yet given the way the EU has evolved, these purely economic reforms are no longer enough. They must be accompanied by a fundamental re-evaluation of the principles which underpin the EU.

Above all, there must be a recognition that the EU philosophically is now being pulled in opposite directions – 'ever closer union' from one side and flexibility from the other. The logical end-point of 'ever closer union' is 'union', while the logical end-point of a more flexible Europe as desired by the people is completely different. Member states are going to have to choose which way they want to go.

Too many people still see the EU from the point of view of the early post-war years. They see only optimism and idealism, and believe that these are all that matter. But we have to realise that the EU of today is a different creature. Europe as a continent has changed, as has the world in which it exists.

Even the Europe of 1995 is no longer the Europe of today. There is tentative peace and stability in the Balkans. One part of the former Yugoslavia, Slovenia, has already joined the European Union. A further nine countries from East Central Europe, the Baltics and the Mediterranean have also joined the organisation. Tens of thousands of young people have travelled from countries such as Poland and the Czech Republic to live and work in London. The latest hot spot for British people to buy foreign property is, apparently, Transylvania in Romania.

This expansion of the EU has also fundamentally changed the nature of the European Union, not least in making English the *lingua franca* of Brussels rather than French. Certainly, I suspect Donald Rumsfeld would never have guessed that his 'old Europe' / 'new Europe' distinction would have become so quickly entrenched in political parlance.

China, south Asia and the Americas continue to take an increased share of the world's market, eroding what could have been, and in the past often was, European prosperity and influence. And it is the changes taking place far beyond Europe's borders which will have the greatest impact on the peoples of the EU. The single biggest determinant of Europe's economic well-being will be how our economies perform relative to countries such as China and India. If we fail to retain competitive advantage, we will pay the price in lost jobs and all which that entails.

Even a rudimentary analysis of China's prospects gives much food for thought. Over the next 25 years, China's economy will grow so rapidly that it is expected to account for more than 20% of the growth in world energy demand.[28] Consumer demand currently is growing seven times faster than the US. Within twenty years, China is set to burn as much oil as the US. More importantly still, its reserves will run out within fourteen years. This cannot but have an impact on Europe and the European economy.

Britain self-evidently needs a Europe which promotes both security and prosperity. To ensure that we can achieve both in today's world, EU reform must be both internal and external – and nobody should argue the case for this more strongly than the Conservative Party. The EU must change the way it does things, but also change the way it sees the world. European leaders need to forge a closer partnership with the United States. Europe needs to turn away from President Chirac's view of the continent in a multi-polar world, by which he wishes to create a Europe apart from and rivalling the US.

In the UK, the Conservative Party must set out the facts and win the argument. We must first demonstrate that it is not possible to support a more flexible Europe and 'ever closer

28 *World Energy Out* 2002, International E Agency.

union' simultaneously. We must acknowledge frankly and honestly that ever closer union is no longer our intent, and that our destiny will never lie in a United States of Europe. In reaching this conclusion, we must recognise that it will have consequences for other unresolved issues, notably whether, and if so how, to complete the Single Market.

It is of paramount importance to the UK economy that the Single Market is completed, and without delay. By and large, there is already a Single Market in goods. By contrast, there is a long way to go on services; Member States are currently considering a Draft Directive on how best to proceed in this area. Given the importance of the service sector to our economy, it is vitally important that the UK Government secures meaningful agreement on completing the Single Market in this area. The Government must devote significant effort to this task and be judged accordingly, and stop wasting time on integrationist projects that the British people neither want nor need. It will be essential to ensure that the final Directive strikes the right balance between furthering the interests of British companies in the service sector and minimising additional encroachment by Brussels into the conduct of business. If the conclusion is that some further regulation is required to ensure the fair and efficient functioning of the Single Market in services, then the goal must be to devise rules which minimise the additional burden on business. If that proves to entail harmonisation, then so be it. However, my strong preference would be for either mutual recognition or the application of national standards.

The future of the EU in general is, of course, traditionally an issue which sharply divides the Conservative and Labour Parties. Never before, however, has that debate been conducted at a time when the stakes are so high. Against the daunting economic backdrop, it is no exaggeration to say that major national interests are at stake. Under such circumstances, politicians of all colours will be well advised to keep those national interests in mind, and to pursue them doggedly.

When there is such an overwhelming imperative for the EU to overhaul its *raison d'etre* and change the way it does business, British politicians of all persuasions should be urging our partners to adopt the British free-market economic model. It is by no means certain, however, whether such good sense will prevail. Hitherto, the Labour Party has tried to talk the language of reform, but continued to pursue greater integration in Europe and greater regulation at home.

There is an argument in some quarters that whether the EU addresses the Lisbon Agenda or not does not really matter to the UK. Since Britain has stayed out of the euro, with the Government having finally come round to the Conservative Party's position, the UK can, on this argument, carry on reaping the benefits of the changes made in the 1980s.

This is a mistake on two counts. First, Labour's economic policies are setting the UK on the same route as over-regulated, over-taxed France and Germany. The Government need to change direction now. If they do not, Britain will pay a huge economic price. Second, what happens in the rest of the EU is important to us because the continent is such a critical trading partner for us.

So long as Labour remains so half-hearted in arguing for economic reform, it falls, as ever, to the Conservative Party to frame and win the arguments. We will have many opportunities to do so, not simply in the conduct of domestic policy but also in our dealings with our friends on the continent, most notably Germany. It is essential that an incoming CDU government in Berlin implements thoroughgoing economic reform. The Conservative Party also shares as much common ground with the Dutch and Danish liberal parties as with some Christian Democrat parties, and far more so than with many of the more protectionist groups on the right of European politics.

Europe must be transformed into a dynamic economy; one that is supple enough to absorb external shocks. The issues at stake are of such magnitude that achieving these goals is not a matter of whether one is on the political right or left. The politics of Europe are far too complex for such a simple dichotomy. Although we may not agree on everything, all supporters of a more free market Europe must work together – wherever they place themselves on the ideological spectrum – to deliver the goals of the Lisbon Agenda. The Conservative Party, working in concert with like-minded parties across Europe, must pursue this new agenda of 'economic freedom'. It is a prize worth winning.

A new theory of the state and a new agenda for public services

Nick Gibb MP

Ideas can spark revolutions and transformations. The power of the ideas put forward by Keith Joseph and Margaret Thatcher still drives forward the most important debates in British politics. But the triumph of conservatism has come at a heavy price for the Conservative Party. Flushed with intellectual victory, it has been unable to come to terms with electoral defeat. It cannot understand how, having won so many of the philosophical arguments, it is Tony Blair's Labour government that is – however timidly – now pursuing and developing so much of the public service policy agenda embarked upon by the Conservatives in the 1980s and 1990s. The unspoken question is, 'if we won the argument, why are we not reaping the rewards of our achievement?'.

To find the answer, Conservatives should look back at why we lost the general election in 1997, and at the problems that the Blair government is encountering in turning reforming rhetoric and policy into the delivery of high quality public services.

1997 was a watershed in British politics. A deeply unpopular Conservative government was swept out of power and replaced by a party promising to deliver real improvements to public services. The Labour critique of Tory reforms in health and education resonated with voters who were fed up with seemingly constant reform without real improvements. Labour said that the Tories would privatise the health service and had little interest in state education. Tony Blair warned there were '24 hours to save the NHS' and promised that 'education, education, education' would be his first three priorities. Reinforced by New Labour's pledge card, the impression given to voters was that, at last, here was a party that would deliver modern, reliable public services for all.

In office – and this is one of the reasons why so many Conservatives passionately dislike Tony Blair's government – New Labour has ended up pursuing precisely the same approach to public service reform as that adopted by the Conservatives from the late 1980s onwards. While New Labour's embrace of the internal market is a cause of despair to many Tories, I believe it presents us with an opportunity to break free from our immediate past, to face up to the fact that internal markets have failed, and instead to develop an alternative agenda to deliver high quality public services within the state sector. It can be done. Whether it is railways and paradors in Spain; the health service in Denmark; the education system in Switzerland; or the police department in New York, around the world are countless examples of high quality public services provided by the state.

The Conservative theory of the state – developed in the mid-1970s in response to a failing and competition-shy British economy – needs updating. The Tory analysis identified the reasons for the failure of nationalisation – lack of competition, poor quality management leaving companies unable to compete with the skills of their international competitors, crippling labour relations problems – and developed a response in the form of privatisation which changed Britain fundamentally and for the better. Privatisation took failing industries out of the hands of politicians and made them accountable to shareholders and to customers.

Accountability is at the heart of the market economy. Businesses are accountable to their shareholders and their customers. Management teams that fail to deliver shareholder value soon find themselves out of work. Companies that fail to satisfy their customers or keep up with their expectations ultimately go bust. Markets work.

But the market based analysis of the 1970s does not provide an adequate roadmap to solve the problems facing the state sector today, which is dominated not by failing corporations, but by two key public services – health and education – that the public have little desire to see in the private sector. Yet Conservative policy at the general election was directed towards finding ways of making the private sector acceptable to voters: policies to enable more and more people to opt-out of the waiting list queue in favour of an operation in the private sector, and, in education, ways to encourage greater diversity of provision of schools (for example by private companies, collectives of parents or charitable institutions). Where privatisation is a no-go area (for example in the ownership of hospitals or the provision of GP services), both Conservatives and Labour remain wedded to the internal market model developed by the Conservatives in government in the 1990s, which was intended to bring the disciplines of the marketplace to the running of public services.

The Conservative reforms – particularly in the health service – were resisted by the professions (not to mention the then Labour opposition) and proved deeply unpopular with the public. Trust hospitals were run by unelected quangos – often selected on the basis of party loyalty rather than expertise or connection to the local community – and the number of managers appeared to mushroom. The efficiencies of the private sector did not appear, and nor did the improved services that voters had been promised.

The internal market model failed to deliver for a very simple reason: it was not a real market. The health reforms were designed to create a structure that would behave as if it were a market, but the trouble with mimicry is that it is not the real thing. Fortunately for Sven-Goran Eriksson, Alistair McGowan is not David Beckham. He might sound like him and – with the help of make-up – even look like him, but he could not stun the Greeks with a perfect, bending free kick in injury time in a match vital for England's qualification for the World Cup finals. Internal markets might look like markets and sometimes behave as markets would behave, but they are not markets.

The failure of internal markets to deliver reform has been precisely because of the absence of the real accountability of the marketplace. Politicians will not let important institutions fail. Internal charging is no substitute for a genuine search through the marketplace for the best-priced goods. Public sector boards (such as those that run hospital trusts) are appointed from a pool of the elite rather than the competent, or drawn from a vast array of different (and often competing) interest groups. Accountability is diffuse and therefore in reality non-existent. What is needed is a new approach, which takes as its starting point the responsibility of politicians to ensure that public services actually deliver what the public expects. It will require a fundamental re-appraisal of the role of politicians in the delivery of the services that voters pay for and care about most. It will require a clear and coherent understanding of the principle of democratic accountability. Above all, it will require politicians to take a much more active role in defining not only what public services should deliver but also how they are delivered. It will involve understanding precisely why our public services are failing to deliver.

In the state sector, accountability for the quality of taxpayer-funded services has to rest with elected politicians. Public services are paid for through taxes set by government. The government is accountable to the people through Parliament. So, if the public are unhappy with the way that a service they pay for through their taxes is run, then their ultimate recourse is to kick out the politicians.

Voters say they want more police on the beat and so politicians of all parties promise more police. The public are allowed to think that that means there will be more officers on the beat but, because chief constables – who have the power to determine how police officers are used – reject the notion that police officers out of cars and on the streets provide a real and visible deterrent, successive governments have actually presided over a decline in the number of officers on the beat (even when, as now, the number of police officers has actually increased). Politicians of all parties promise to raise education standards but in government confine their reforms to structural changes aimed at creating diversity and choice, rather than engage in debate about what and how children are taught.

And in health, clear though it is to the public that the problem with the NHS is its appalling management, politicians have not set out to establish proper modern management methods but instead have proposed reform to the structure, which will increase the diffuse, and therefore unaccountable, nature of the NHS.

If politicians are not prepared to question the way that police forces operate, then what can the public do to influence policing? If politicians will not take a view about different teaching methods, then what can parents do to ensure their children are being properly educated? It is simply not a good enough answer to say – as most Conservatives would – that a market mechanism will deliver. We have enough experience of internal markets to know that real markets work; pretend ones do not.

Politicians must stop evading their responsibilities. If the public is going to get the public services it wants, then politicians are going to have to stop passing the buck and face up to the fact that they have an important role to play in ensuring that taxpayer funded services are delivered to the highest possible quality.

The efficacy of current policing methods is a policy matter. It needs to be assessed by examination of the data, policing methods in other countries, and policy trends in this country. It cannot be left only to the police to decide. The public must have a say, and politicians are the public's representatives. In education, it is time for politicians to engage in debate about teaching methods as well as structure. It is a policy matter when, for example, methods for the teaching of reading result in worse literacy levels in this country than elsewhere. Of course, the views and advice of experts should be fully and properly taken into account, but ultimately – in a publicly funded system – accountability rests with politicians.

Many people argue that the answer is to decentralise the delivery of public services. It is argued that what is best for people living in one part of the country is not necessarily best for those living elsewhere. Local communities, it is suggested, should be able to set their own priorities. Localism is, however, built on a myth and an old-fashioned view of the way that modern, dynamic organisations operate.

A caricature of Britain's public services has emerged. It is argued by politicians of all parties that the 1980s and 1990s saw an unprecedented shift of power away from local communities towards central government. The reality is different. The National Health Service, for example, is made up of over

600 separate organisations, each accountable to its own local board and each with its own chief executive. The Secretary of State for Health, and even the so-called Chief Executive of the NHS (who is in reality the Permanent Secretary of the Department of Health), has virtually no direct executive power in the management of any of these 600 organisations. His influence relies upon the issuing of targets and guidelines, which through skewing priorities can often have damaging effects elsewhere.

Education too is highly dispersed. Heads of state schools are appointed by independent, locally appointed governors. Funding – although largely provided by central government – is channelled through local education authorities (which, although theoretically accountable to local electors, are not themselves directly elected, but are made up of local councillors who are often elected in very low turnout elections dominated more by national politics than by truly local issues). LEAs and their advisers have considerably more influence over what is taught in schools than central government. The Secretary of State for Education has very little real executive power over the state education system and so – like his counterpart in the NHS – relies on targets, guidelines and inspections in order to exert influence. And as with the NHS, education targets have had distorting and deleterious effects. Targets for attainment in schools, for example, have led to a reduction in exam standards, and teachers at primary level 'teaching to the test'.

The police too are highly dispersed. Most counties have their own police force or else have a joint force with a neighbouring county or unitary authority. Each police force is accountable to a police committee, which, like LEAs, are made up of representatives from the relevant local authorities. The Home Secretary, therefore, has very little direct control over policing decisions.

The problem with Britain's public services is not that they are too centralised. It is that they are often badly run and do not reflect (to use a New Labour soundbite) the people's priorities. As a result, and in the light of constant criticism from the public, politicians of all parties have resorted to setting targets and finding ways of exerting more direct control over funding mechanisms. The answer is not to localise them – which would only have the effect of making accountability still more diffuse – but to learn lessons from the way that the world's best managed organisations are run.

The key is management. The establishment of clear objectives and, based on experience, systems and processes, to deliver those objectives most effectively. An international firm of accountants will have a clear set of objectives: to provide high quality audits and financial advice to clients. In delivering these objectives, it will have established clear procedures and methodology that local managers are expected to adopt while also giving local managers wide-ranging responsibilities and discretion to reflect local market conditions.

In health, politicians need to establish clearly the objectives of the health service, of hospitals, of GP clinics, and establish modern management methods – tried and tested in large organisations worldwide – to ensure these objectives are delivered. Hospital building, IT systems, and hospital appointment systems should all be nationally established processes; pay and conditions a matter for local discretion as well as the range and style of services, reflecting local needs. The Royal College of Physicians and the Royal College of Surgeons both have similar best practice guidelines on the medical side, the area of the NHS least criticised.

In education too, politicians need to establish the objective – providing the highest quality education to all our children – and they need to engage with the professionals to establish best practice in the delivery of this objective. International data clearly demonstrates that teaching children to read using synthetic phonics exclusively is significantly more effective than the long-standing British method of 'look and say', or a combination of both. In Britain 23% of adults cannot read properly compared to 7% in Sweden, which uses synthetic phonics.[29] I am not arguing for politicians to impose such methods on a recalcitrant profession, but to engage with the profession in discussing these matters and, ultimately, to make the decision. The same applies to mixed ability teaching. 60% of lessons in secondary schools take place in classes of mixed ability, and yet our comprehensive schools do not appear to be delivering the type and standard of education demanded by parents and which is vital to Britain's ability to compete in the global marketplace.

...t just the leader - we ed a new direction, dian, October 2003.

Employers complain of poorly educated school leavers, and in reliable international comparisons Britain ranks 20th out of 41 OECD countries in terms of its standard of education.[30]

In crime policy, politicians again need to establish the objective – obviously that of reducing crime – and engage in examining policing methods which are proven to be most effective. This is an area in which Conservatives have found it acceptable to research – looking closely at policing methods in New York.

The lesson here is that politicians need to be engaged in the 'nitty gritty' of the issues that are the causes of the failure of these public services: in health, the poor management; in education, the use of outmoded teaching methods that fail by international comparison; in crime, policing policy that also fails when compared to the best examples internationally. Politicians need to abandon their obsession with structural reform designed to bring about such change through indirect methods. The Conservatives, in particular, need to abandon their obsession with the invisible hand of the free market and actually develop policies for running these public services within the state sector.

None of this agenda excludes the introduction of more choice in the range of schools or hospitals available, nor does it preclude tax incentives for health insurance or subsidies for those who opt for private sector treatment. Choice is a good thing. It is, however, about accepting that such policies will not of themselves drive up standards within the state sector. It is about accepting that there are no formulaic panaceas (localism, the internal market) that will push up standards. Politicians (particularly Conservative politicians) need to address the real and particular causes of the problems of state sector provision and, by doing so successfully, they may even begin to restore the public's faith in the processes of democratic accountability.

---

30 PISA 2003, OECD International Association the Evaluation of Edu Achievement the third national maths and s study (1995).

Better public services the modern Conservative way

Damian Green MP

Those who wish to see the Conservative Party flourish through a transformation of its attitudes to the modern world must themselves be outward looking. The internal processes and culture of the Party are vitally important but, while they are a matter of undying fascination to a small minority of insiders, they are completely irrelevant to the mass of the population. Indeed a Party obsessed with itself is by definition failing to engage properly with the world.

'Modernisation' must mean wanting to produce a modern Tory Britain, not just a modern Tory Party. Central to this is the need to provide a new way of providing decent healthcare, education, and other services. The defeatist view that 'these are Labour issues' needs to be challenged not just because nothing is immutable in politics (look at Labour's economic reputation before Gordon Brown), but because if the British people think an issue is permanently important then a political party which ignores it is flirting with irrelevance.

Creating a modern Tory alternative on these issues does not entail starting from pure theory, since comparable countries around Europe and the rest of the world set a variety of examples from which Britain can choose. Indeed one of the most liberating changes the Conservative Party could take would be to stop looking at public sector issues through the prism of twentieth century politics. The old left wing view that more money equals better services has been discredited, but so has the old right wing dogma of 'private sector good, public sector bad'. Competition, choice, and consumer power – all good

Conservative principles – will need to be at the heart of better provision, but simply hoping to replicate private sector structures in all public services will not work. There is a legitimate public demand for equity in access to these services which simply does not exist for private sector goods, so the provision of competition and choice needs to be achieved in different ways.

So a modern Conservative solution will have to avoid being Old Labour or Old Thatcherite, but will also have to be distinctive from New Labour. The New Labour rhetoric of 'more money accompanied by reform' has been seductive, but too often the reform has not been pushed through. The stated desire in both health and education has been to give more responsibility to front-line staff, but combining this with a plethora of central targets has proved impossible.

The two main public services, health and education, show that the defining characteristic of this country after eight years of New Labour government is that its public services provide bad value. Since 1998-99, current spending on schools has increased by 42%, and capital expenditure has doubled. But the international PISA study which compares standards across countries shows us falling back in the basic subjects, and the House of Commons Education and Skills Select Committee has pointed out that the improvement in GCSE grades since 1997 is almost exactly the same as it was in the years before then, when spending was largely static in real terms. Health spending has risen 42% in real terms since 1999, but the OECD said last year that: 'in the health sector there are few indicators showing unambiguous improvements in outcomes over and above trend improvements that were already apparent before the surge in spending'.[32]

Clearly, there is scope for a radical and compassionate alternative. But if we reject the intellectually easy but practically wrong (and politically suicidal) option of 'privatise the lot' then we need a set of principles to guide us. Beyond the principles, different structural solutions are needed in each of the services, not least because of the different demands we make on the various services. For example, education demand for each household is predictable and long lasting, whereas healthcare demand can be both unexpected and potentially enormous. Household demand for transport can be much more a matter of choice. So

31 House of Commons Education and Skills Committee *Public Expenditure* First Report of Session 2004–05 (2005) London The Stationery Office

32 OECD Economic January 2004.

there is no simple over-arching blueprint for all the various services.

The guiding principles for public service reform that I would propose are:

- no-one should be denied access to decent education or healthcare because of their economic or social circumstances;
- the state's duty is to ensure universal access, not to provide the services except where necessary to ensure availability;
- any subsidy given to individuals to buy essential services should also support the infrastructure of universal provision;
- alternative providers should be actively encouraged, and should be used particularly to provide services to the most disadvantaged;
- extra subsidies may be given to individuals who suffer from particular disadvantages or needs;
- there should be less prescription about the way of delivering a service, as long as the outcomes are satisfactory.

These principles would produce a radically different system, in which alternative providers would compete for customers, each of whom would be given consumer power by state subsidy. This subsidy would be provided in a different way for each service, but the overall effect will be the creation of strong, well-funded and universally available systems. Of course the option of purely private provision would remain. The issue of 'co-payment' will be dealt with in the individual sectors below. What I do not advocate is the option of encouraging people to opt out if they can, since this reduces the universally available services to providers of last resort.

One other core point is that these reforms need to be accompanied by visible improvements in the daily lives of those using the services affected. It must be easy for the users to see what instant changes will emerge. Otherwise, there will be a political battle between those promoting apparently theoretical improvements in the long-term and others offering an immediate concrete change – a battle which it would be difficult to win. Those at the bottom of the socio-economic heap, who, especially in education, have to put up with the worst service, would be more tempted by radical change than those who think things could be better but are on the whole happy to rub along with what is currently on offer. This latter group, used to being offered mediocrity but unsure that a state-funded system can aspire any higher, will be the most difficult to convince.

In education, radical reforms can build on some of the rhetoric, if not the reality, of the Blair years. The Labour Government has promised greater diversity and parental choice. A Conservative Government would deliver excellent education in all areas by accepting two propositions: that money can be released to be spent as parents want, in the classroom, by significant pruning of the apparatus of central control, and that provision which is both excellent and fair can be achieved by giving parents direct control over the funding. This would involve a reform of the supply, in that new bodies would be encouraged to set up or take over 'state' schools, with a much greater diversity of the type of education offered. It would also involve a transformation of the funding mechanism, with each child given a block of funding to cover both revenue and capital costs.

Let us take the operation of the supply side first. One of the most arresting discoveries I made during my time as Shadow Education Secretary was that countries whose whole political spectrum is well to the left of Britain's, such as Sweden and Holland, have education systems which would seem to the British education establishment to have sprung from the wilder ideas of right-wing think tanks. In Holland, any group that can sign up the requisite number of pupils to make a particular school viable has the right to be given state funding to do so. As a result, over 70% of Dutch children are educated in independent schools, although none of them are paying fees.[33]

Similarly in Sweden, the introduction of a general voucher system (of which more below) has led to a proliferation of independent school providers. From a position in the early 1990s where there were simply no independent schools, some areas are now seeing around 20% of pupils in the independent (but again not fee-paying) sector.[34]

The great prize for a modernising Conservative Government would be to expand the chance of an excellent education that is often available to those who can pay for it to everyone else. We are seeing the first signs of independent education being offered at fee levels close to the state capitation fee. If that fee was available from every child in the country

33 See Eurodice Da[...] for full description of Dutch School system

34 Clowes, G: "Strap Armor and Go: Never In!" *School Reform N* June 1, 1998 The He[...] Institute.

many new providers would emerge, but the existence of general parental choice would force the operators to provide what parents want – which will of course differ from school to school. So real diversity will be built into the system.

As for the funding, it would be possible to move to a universal voucher system in one move, as the Swedes did. Another option would be to roll this out, starting with the big cities where the problems are most acute. This would have the advantage of providing the chance for new schools to come first where they are most needed. The existence of hundreds of supplementary schools in our inner cities, where children receive extra tuition on Saturdays, often organised by faith groups for ethnic minority groups, shows that the demand for an excellent education is as prevalent in the inner cities as it is in the suburbs.

Some of the American experiments with vouchers have been versions of this, with the voucher targeted specifically at low-income families. Another attractive version allows higher levels of payment for certain children, either because they have special needs or because they wish to pursue vocational courses which need equipment that is more expensive. This kind of variable voucher acts as a preventative measure against the development of sink schools, as more difficult children can bring more funding with them, making them more desirable to schools.

The role of central and local government would be to provide schooling where operators were not available; to offer services such as transport which schools may not be able to organise themselves; and most importantly to provide parents with clear and independent information about the performance of schools based on a system of independent inspection. The National Curriculum could be cut back to its essentials, and most of the targets and guidelines could go.

As for further and higher education, similar principles could apply. Vocational courses are often more expensive than academic ones, so could attract higher levels of individual funding. It would also be possible to set up a variable voucher system for higher education; with higher A Level grades attracting higher levels of funding. This would enable universities to create a proper market in the price of their degrees without the problems associated with co-payment, which leaves the most desirable universities more available to those from affluent backgrounds who are less deterred by large debt levels.

Just as many other countries have been keen to allow greater diversity and freedom within the state-funded education system than we have, so few other countries attempt to fund and deliver healthcare with an institution as all embracing as the National Health Service.

Hindering the development of a rational debate about health policy in the UK has been the myth that the NHS is the 'envy of the world'. We have grown out of that delusion, but not out of the emotional attachment to the institution. The delusional nature of our attachment can be illustrated by any number of comparative figures. We have less than half the number of practising physicians per 1000 population than Germany;[35] our life expectancy is lower than that of Spain, Italy, or Greece;[36] and the uptake of new drugs in the NHS has been a third that of the French system[37].

There are three ways in which advanced countries fund healthcare: out of taxation, a social insurance system, or a voluntary private insurance system. The problems with the tax-based NHS system are manifold and obvious; it has no responsiveness to individual demands; it has to ration purely by waiting time; and as health demands rise it is increasingly unaffordable. To match the spending levels of the more advanced EU economies would require tax rises equivalent to a VAT rate of 27%.[38]

35 Hansard, Nov 20 Column 265W, answe Secretary of State for

36 See *EU Statistics Focus*, theme 3 17/2

37 Reform, *Quick Br Health Needs Reform* 2003.

38 Appelby & Boyle Blair's billions: where find the money for th *BMJ*, 2000, 320, pp 867.

We have less than half the number of practising physicians per 1000 population than Germany; our life expectancy is lower than that of Spain, Italy, or Greece; and the uptake of new drugs in the NHS has been a third that of the French system.

So the system is broken and needs fixing. A modern Tory solution should be careful not to replace chronic inefficiency with palpable unfairness. The ultimate cause of the problems in the NHS is lack of capacity. Not only do we spend the money inefficiently but we do not spend enough in the first place. Given that we do not want to see huge rises in taxation, we need to promote a better system of funding which would lead to the necessary increase in capacity. We need to do this in different ways from before, so that we do not seem to be concerned only with those who are able to help themselves. We do not want to subsidise the relatively affluent to remove themselves from the waiting lists by going elsewhere for treatment, even though that would relieve a small amount of the pressure, because that would lay us open to the damaging charge of being concerned mainly with the well off.

The long-term solution lies in an insurance-based system; whether private or 'social' (the latter includes employer contributions). The key aspect of any insurance system should be that it is compulsory. The voluntary system in the USA leaves behind many of the poor and elderly, as well the chronically unhealthy who cannot afford insurance. Most European countries use social insurance systems, but the Swiss have a highly regarded private system, with the key element of compulsion and therefore universal cover. As long as there are competing insurers then the system will be responsive and flexible. Most importantly, the added money that would come in through people's direct insurance contributions would enable an expansion of national capacity, at the same time demonstrating that the best treatment is still available to all based on clinical need. Clearly, the Government would subsidise those who simply cannot afford the insurance premiums, whether temporarily or permanently.

Within this new funding structure, it would also be sensible to remove large amounts of the current central control and target setting. Hospitals would run better with less outside control, and so would GPs. The insurance systems would cover an agreed comprehensive package of essential services (which would change over time and would itself be a tough job to define) so that no-one need worry what would happen in an emergency, or if a very expensive problem arose.

If the Conservative Party adopted the principles and policies I have advocated here, then it would be taking three steps forward. First, it would show that it was committed to improving the public sector in a way that would be unthinkable for any other party in Britain. Conservative modernisation of schools and hospitals would entail a serious reform in the direction of individual power. It would be a powerful statement that in an era when technology has handed power back to the individual and the small group, the facts of life are once again Tory.

Second, it would lead to a change in perceptions of the Conservative Party. It would show that the Party realises the importance of non-economic values, and recognises that there is more to life than markets; more to successful politics than hard-nosed economics.

The third benefit of these reforms would be in highlighting the difference between the Blair Government and a reforming Conservative Party. They would show that the modern Tory Party is not just about cutting back the size of the state; it is about making the vital services funded by the state better. It is not about encouraging people to opt out from bad services, but instead to produce modern structures so that public services can be excellent. Much of this has been foreshadowed by New Labour rhetoric, but little of it has been delivered. So the Conservative promise would not be to go back to any golden era; it would be to move on from the Blair era, making a reality of the promises he and the Labour Party could not deliver.

Direct democracy: a radical agenda for change

Douglas Carswell MP

May 2005, and a third election disaster for the Conservative Party. Once again, the Party started a new Parliament with fewer MPs than Labour in 1983. Despite gaining 33 more seats, the Party increased its share of the popular vote by slightly over half of one percent. In 1997, the Conservatives secured 30.7% of the vote. In 2001, 31.7%. In 2005, 32.3%. At this rate of progress, it will be the year 2037 before the Tories can even hope to form a Parliamentary majority. What has the Party been doing wrong?

Since the election, strategists from all three parties have accepted that, on the ground, the Tories had the best of it. In 2005, after eighteen years of being out-performed, the Conservatives leap-frogged the other two parties in their use of demographic identification, direct mailing and targeting. Yet it made little difference.

Nor was it a question of leadership. Tony Blair will soon be on his fifth Opposition Leader. Neither a new leader nor 'one more heave' will be enough to secure a Parliamentary majority, since the reasons for people's rejection of the Conservatives run deeper. The Party's most profound failing since the late 1980s has been a lack of ideas. A lack of an overriding critique of the problems that beset contemporary Britain, and thus a lack of a coherent and compelling set of policies to demonstrate that the Party is capable of forming a government that would deal with them.

The Conservatives failed to convince in the run-up to the 2005 election because their policies lacked coherence, and any overriding vision of what the Party stood for. That is not to say the Party lacked policies; indeed, the Party had policies on everything from fly-tipping to MRSA. Yet, like Churchill's pudding, it had no theme.

Even when boiled down to 'five pledges' during the campaign, the Party's polices were seemingly ad-hoc pronouncements that had been approved by focus group. That the Party stood for 'cleaner hospitals', 'school discipline' or 'more police' was not enough – which party wanted anything different? The Party failed to show how it would deliver on these pledges.

When the Conservatives were last in opposition in the late 1970s, Keith Joseph, Alfred Sherman and others developed an integral critique of what was wrong with Britain. Their critique provided the Party with the policy response, in what became Thatcherism, that addressed not merely the immediate problems Britain faced during the 'winter of discontent', but an intellectual compass that guided the Party to the correct response even when facing new challenges outside their immediate experience. The Party had grasped that Britain's problem was excessive state control over the economy. It therefore had a predisposition towards sweeping away constraints on the citizen.

Far from advocating re-heated Thatcherism, the Party must today recognise that the doctrine that fed and sustained the Conservatives after 1979 was a specific reaction to specific conditions. Indeed, as Thatcherism addressed those conditions, and transformed Britain, the Party attempted to keep living off its increasingly stale intellectual capital. If the problem with Britain in 1979 was one of the command economy, today it is one of the command state. Then, unelected trade union bosses suborned the British economy. Today, unelected apparatchiks have suborned British democracy from within the machinery of the state.

Most of the problems in contemporary Britain – hospitals that infect patients; schools that do not teach properly; policemen who do not go after criminals; and immigration authorities who will not remove illegal immigrants – are caused by a massive centralisation of power around remote and unaccountable institutions. Centralisation – aggrandisement of power by remote elites at the expense of individuals and local communities – has been driven by targets imposed by Whitehall; the central funding of public services with ever-more strings attached; the growth of quangos; and judicial activism. It is difficult to think of any area of policy that has not been subjected to dozens of 'plans', 'strategies' and 'public service agreements'. Centrally allocated funding allows Whitehall to demand compliance over how public services are run. Unprecedented powers are wielded by bodies that, while part of the state machine, are outside of the spotlight of democratic accountability.

It is tempting to blame all of these developments on New Labour – and much of that blame would be merited. Yet the problem runs far deeper than any one party. During the 1980s, it was Tory ministers who were rate-capping local authorities; imposing the National Curriculum on schools; setting NHS targets; and strengthening the control of the Home Office over local police forces.

The ability of democratically elected MPs and Councillors to influence decisions that affected people's lives has diminished substantially. Far from being apathetic, non-voters recognise that those whose names appear on the ballot paper have been rendered increasingly powerless by an over-mighty executive; an undemocratic EU; activist judges; and other forces. As our system of representative democracy has given way to a system of post-representative democracy, more and more people have come to realise that there is often little point in voting for a representative at all. As Lord Butler, Head of the Civil Service from 1988 to 1998, put it:

> All decisions are delegated by politicians, because politicians don't want to take responsibility for them, to quangos, and quangos aren't answerable to anybody. Now what can you really hold politicians responsible for?[39]

It should hardly surprise us that voters regard politicians as 'all the same', promising the earth but never delivering, when the truth is that politicians have so little discretion to alter policies formulated by health experts, educationalists, human rights lawyers, police authorities, and Brussels. The rising public disenchantment with politicians is a measure of their inability to decide on the things in life that matter to the electorate. Politicians promise, but remote elites actually decide. The actions of their local council, or of the House of Commons, often has less impact on them than that of the Highways

Agency; the Child Support Agency; the National Institute for Clinical Excellence; Primary Care Trusts; the Health and Safety Executive; and hundreds of other such quangos.

How can we place power back in the hands of local people? Several other countries operate systems based on localism and direct democracy. Two outstanding examples – one much smaller than the UK and one many times bigger – are Switzerland and the United States. In their different ways, both states respect the principles of the dispersal of power, the direct election of public officials and the use of referendums as a legislative tool. Likewise in the UK, power could be pushed down to the individual where possible and, failing that, to the Town Hall. Lawmakers could be made more directly accountable and the citizen would enjoy maximum freedom from state control. Measures to secure this goal include:

Setting town halls free

Local councils should be made self-financing; a pre-requisite for genuine local democracy. This could chiefly be achieved by replacing VAT with a Local Sales Tax (LST) to be levied by County or Metropolitan Councils.

Local government's fiscal autonomy is the starting point for a wholesale transfer of powers and responsibilities to local government. Broadly, areas of policy currently run by the office of the Deputy Prime Minister could be devolved fully to local government. Those elected to serve in town halls would decide the location of mobile phone masts, set local taxes and make other decisions central to their local community, rather than merely rubber-stamping decisions made at the centre.

With 75% of the money spent by local councils coming from the Treasury, there is little link between taxation, representation and expenditure at local level. This has the perverse effect of rewarding inefficient councils, eroding accountability, diminishing choice (since political parties cease to be able to offer radically different manifestos) and alienating voters. It also deters many good candidates from standing for local government since someone standing for local government must be willing to be micro-managed by a distant bureaucracy.

By happy coincidence, VAT happens to raise for central government almost the same amount – £64bn – as it hands over to local councils in grants – £66bn. So devolving the power to tax goods and services to town halls would not be an additional levy; rather it would replace an existing and highly unpopular tax. Unlike VAT, which is complicated and expensive to administer, the LST would be charged just once, at the point of retail. It would be set at the level of a county or metropolitan authority, and local councils would be free to vary the rate according to their spending needs. The effect of this would be tax competition, keeping rates down and forcing councils to be as efficient as possible in utilising tax pounds to provide services.

While self-financing town halls would have many powers devolved to them, in some cases, the aim of local accountability would be better served by having a single directly elected official, such as in policing.

Sending for the sheriff

Crime is one the public's main concerns, and yet people are immune to politicians' promises of 'more police'. The challenge is to explain how a party will actually reduce crime.

Appointed and impotent police authorities should be replaced with directly elected sheriffs, with real power to direct local police forces' priorities. Sheriffs should also have responsibility for supervising public prosecutions in place of the Crown Prosecution Service, and punishments in place of the Probation Service. Sheriffs would appoint and dismiss Chief Constables, make their own policing plan, and control their own budgets, allocated to them as a block grant. They would answer to local voters for their effectiveness in spending that money in the fight against crime.

Freeing our education system

Britain's education system is failing. The value of exam grades is falling and bad behaviour is now endemic. Yet no party has succeeded in convincing voters that things will improve under its watch.

The Conservatives should adopt a policy of radical localisation. Schools should become independent, freestanding institutions with full control over their staffing and pupil rolls. New providers should be allowed to enter the market and compete for pupils. Parents should have the automatic right to request and receive funding for their child's education from their (self-financing) local council, and take this money to a school of their choice. Parents, rather than here-today-gone-tomorrow politicians, would be the driving force shaping our education system. It would be them, not politicians, who would demand, and get, school discipline.

Introducing meaningful choice in health

Britain already has one of the most expensive health services in the world, yet one that still fails to meet public expectations. The problem with the NHS is not resources, but the fact it is a state-run monopoly established over half a century ago.

Transferring power over the NHS from national to local politicians would do little to address its endemic flaws. Instead, the aim must be to empower the patient. We should fund patients, either through the tax system or by way of universal insurance, to purchase health care from the provider of their choice. The state would continue to guarantee care for all, yet it would lose its monopoly to provide that care where it could be provided better elsewhere.

Modernising our constitution

New Labour has repeatedly embarked on constitutional projects – a Supreme Court, Lords reform, the Human Rights Act, English Regionalism – without any clear objective. The Conservative Party's aim, by contrast, must be to propose specific solutions to identified problems.

Britain already has one of the most expensive health services in the world, yet one that still fails to meet public expectations. The problem with the NHS is not resources, but the fact it is a state-run monopoly established over half a century ago.

Parliament's authority has seeped out in four main directions: to Ministers, to quangos, to judges and to the EU. Each leakage has drained away some of the popular consent necessary in a democratic system. Restoring the legitimacy of our political institutions must entail placing powers in the hands of elected representatives who are vulnerable to public opinion.

Humbling the judiciary

The readiness of judges to take political decisions – that is, to rule based on what they think the law ought to say, rather than what it actually says – is not peculiar to Britain. In almost every democracy, the judiciary has sought to expand its powers beyond what the legislature has laid down. The problem with judicial activism is that there is, by definition, no legislative prophylactic against it. MPs can insert whatever safeguards they want, but if the court dislikes a statute it will simply ignore their safeguards. What then can be done? First, the judicial process should be subject to the same principles of decentralisation and democracy that have guided us throughout. This means specifically that the powers currently controlled by the CPS would be placed at the disposal of a local Sheriff who would, furthermore, have the right to set sentencing guidelines (although not interfere in individual cases).

Second, there should be a degree of democratic control over judicial appointments. There needs to be a process of transparent parliamentary hearings to confirm senior appointments to the judiciary rather than, as at present, having senior judges nominated by the Lord Chancellor or, as is now proposed, a government appointment panel.

Finally, the authority of Parliament should be stated explicitly in a Reserve Powers Act that would delineate a number of areas where MPs' decisions were supreme. This would be a defence, not so much against domestic judicial activism, as against the encroachment of foreign jurisdictions. The European Court of Justice has a hunger for power that surpasses even the most activist British judge, and has repeatedly pushed its authority beyond what is written in European treaties.

Constraining the executive

As the powers of the legislature have dwindled, those of the executive have increased. It is surely worth standing back for a moment and asking whether it is right for the Prime Minister to have the degree of patronage that he now has. It would close the democratic deficit somewhat if the powers currently exercised under crown prerogative – the appointment of heads of executive agencies and commissions, and also perhaps Foreign Office postings – were transferred to Parliament deliberated over in open hearings.

In the same spirit, the treaty-making powers of the Prime Minister, also exercised under crown prerogative, should be transferred to Parliament. If it were impractical to insist on this procedure for every single accord, it should at the very least apply where a foreign treaty imposes significant domestic obligations on Britain: NATO, the European Convention on Human Rights, and so on.

Bolstering the legislature

Finally, there are a number of reforms that the House of Commons could implement to strengthen its legitimacy *vis-à-vis* the electorate. These ideas are indicative, rather than comprehensive.

At the beginning of each Parliamentary session, having read out her Government's proposed legislation, the Queen should then turn to her people's bills: legislative proposals that have attracted a certain number of petition signatures and so earned themselves the right to be debated and voted on. There would be no obligations on MPs to pass these proposals, but they would have to take sides and then justify their position to their constituents.

The composition of the House of Lords is impossible to reconcile with the principle of Direct Democracy. Indeed, a largely appointed chamber is the worst of all imaginable options. Whatever the individual qualities of the current chamber's members, it is made up of people who can pass laws without having to justify themselves to those who must obey their laws. An ideal Upper House would have a measure of democratic legitimacy but not one which challenged the primacy of the House of Commons nor which created a completely new tier of politicians. How to constitute such a chamber merits a more detailed study, but one idea would be to bring together a geographically and politically representative selection of existing elected figures. For instance, we could constitute an Upper House of seconded county and borough councillors in proportion to their party's representation in each shire or city. Such a body would correct the metropolitan bias of the current chamber.

Reigning in the European Union
The Conservative Party's approach to European integration should flow naturally from its domestic agenda. If we want decisions to be taken as close as possible to the people they affect, they plainly should not be made in Brussels. If we prefer Direct Democracy to unelected quangos, we can hardly subject ourselves to the biggest quango of the lot, the European Commission. If we believe in personal liberty and accountable, clean government, then we cannot be part of what the EU is becoming. Indeed, a number of the policies set out in this chapter – replacing VAT with LST, a Reserve Powers Act – are incompatible with EU law.

If Britain is to be a democratic country, it cannot accept the supremacy of regulations passed by unaccountable functionaries. The Reserve Powers Act should specify that the policies stemming from foreign treaty obligations would come into force only following their specific implementation by Parliament; and sections 2 and 3 of the European Communities Act should be repealed to the same end.

Far from being faddish ideas, Direct Democracy and localism offer the British centre-right an answer to their greatest strategic problem: namely, the fact that a left-leaning liberal elite has successfully taken control of those institutions responsible for almost every aspect of life in Britain today. Those who doubt this must ask themselves a few diagnostic questions, like: why do judges appear to always rule against the removal of illegal immigrants, rather than for their deportation? What is it about our criminal justice system that makes it softer and more tolerant of criminals than most citizens would wish? Why does the BBC or the Arts Council tend to use taxpayers money to promote left-leaning views of Britain and the world? Why is it that the Foreign Office mandarins seem inherently better at negotiating away British sovereignty (think of the attempts to secure joint-sovereignty over Gibraltar) than at defending it (remember Maastricht and the proposed EU constitution)? How is it that even Conservative-run local authorities use taxpayers' money to promote inherently interventionist and un-Conservative 'economic regeneration' programmes, or impose the leftist dogma of 'inclusion' on special needs children? Why is the default setting for almost every institution in Britain today left-of-centre?

The success of the left cannot be measured purely in terms of the majorities passing through the divisions of the House of Commons, but in terms of their long march through the institutions of public life. As the Marxist intellectual Antonio Gramsci foresaw, the left would be able successfully to impose its views only by achieving a cultural hegemony over public institutions. The right response must be not merely to focus on securing a parliamentary majority, for this will almost certainly be insufficient, but to fundamentally reshape and thereby retake the institutions captured by the left through a radical programme of Direct Democracy.

Make the town halls; criminal justice system; schools and health care services; the Foreign Office, and just about every other leftist institution presiding over public life more directly democratically accountable, and their default setting will have to start reflecting not the latest dogmas of the left-leaning liberal elite, but the views of the British people. Under the harsh spotlight of accountability to the taxpayer, citizen, parent and patient, the profligacy of local councils, ineffectualness of the criminal justice system, woolly-mindedness of the educational 'experts', blatant activism of the judges, and unpatriotism of Whitehall's mandarins would all be exposed and ultimately overturned.

Raising standards: getting the basics rights

David Cameron MP

Five years ago, the Government launched an advertising campaign to recruit teachers. The ads had a simple and true message: 'no-one forgets a good teacher'. Of all the influences on our lives, few are as profound as a good teacher. Teaching is more than a profession; it is a vocation. It is a calling to make the world a better place by working with the young to enrich their minds. That is why the state has to invest in teaching, and compete in the market to get the best possible teachers. The labour market and the quality of our social fabric depend on the quality of our teachers and of what they teach. As a recent SMF paper stated, our 'sophisticated economy is increasingly dependent not on its fund of physical capital but on its capacity to mobilise the brainpower of its citizens'. A decent education is the best start in life that any child can have, and gives a chance for everyone – whatever their background – to better themselves. If we want to create a genuine opportunity society and are determined to unlock human potential, and if we believe that every life is precious and no-one should have their chance to contribute written off, then we have to reform our education system.

For many children in state schools, especially those born with the fewest advantages in life, there has been a persistent failure to believe in their right to the best. They have been held back by what George Bush senior called the 'soft bigotry of low expectations'. We still have not built an education system which genuinely meets the needs of the disadvantaged. In some ways, we have actually made it worse. The goal of an opportunity society is receding from our grasp. Thirty years ago, two-thirds of the students attending Oxford and Cambridge were from state schools. Today, just half are from state schools.

The importance of education goes much further than ensuring social mobility. Our failure to build a state education system which leaves no child behind has contributed to a society in which young lives are unnecessarily blighted. Would so many teenage girls get pregnant if they had been inspired at school; taught to be ambitious for themselves; and equipped with the right skills to go out and get a job? Would so many young men turn away from a life of responsibility, and towards anti-social behaviour, if they were taught to read properly so that they could see the point of education rather than view it as something between a waste of time and a source of embarrassment? The connection between illiteracy and crime is evident: almost 70% of our now record prison population cannot read or write properly.

There is a link between a poverty of expectation, poverty in society, and the reality of thousands of scarred lives. Tackling the roots of these social problems depends on making a success of our education system. We need to reform education to equip future generations for an ever more competitive world: in the age of globalisation, the future is bleaker than ever for those without skills, but opportunities are richer than ever for those with them.

Politicians have an important role to play. We can facilitate an environment in which achieving these things is easier than at present, and we can also make sure that we do not argue over things on which we fundamentally agree, just because the people we are agreeing with are in another party. Where there is political consensus, we should celebrate it: the Government wants a diversity of schools and is considering devolving greater power to heads and governors. Many in the Conservative Party have always shared this goal. Where these things actually happen, many will applaud and support them.

Yet where things are still going wrong, where the Government is failing to give the right lead, or where it fails to deliver on promises – and there are plenty of such areas – the Conservatives must take a stand and try to build a new consensus. In recent times, party political debate has often been in danger of missing the big point in education. The Labour Party has talked primarily about 'resources': spending per pupil, per school, and as a share of our national wealth. The Conservative Party has talked more about 'structures', giving parents greater choices between different sorts of schools. Both are important – but this may overlook the vital element of what actually happens in our state schools. Will our children learn to read, write and add up properly? Will they be safe in class? Will they be stretched to the best of their abilities? Will they be taught the skills they need to have a successful career when they leave? These are the questions parents ask themselves and worry most about when considering their children's education. That is why our focus should be simple and straightforward – on the basics such as discipline; standards; the promotion of teaching methods that work and the scrapping of those that do not; the building on tests, league tables and exam standards that genuinely measure success, failure and progress; and the removal of those that dumb down, promote an 'all must have prizes mentality' or simply waste time.

It is only once we have established what constitutes a good education that we should go on to ask: what stands in its way? How can we clear the obstacles in its path? There are five main areas of weakness in education: literacy in primary schools; discipline in secondary schools; Special Educational Needs; the fact that bright children are being left out and non-academic children are left behind; and a system for testing and examining that – put simply – is currently not fit for the task at hand. I will consider these areas in turn.

In spite of progress made by the national literacy strategy, around one in five children leaves primary school unable to read properly, and one in three leaves without being able to write properly. If you cannot read, you cannot learn. These children are lost to education. The waste – for them, for our country – is nothing short of a scandal.

The evidence that traditional teaching methods – particularly synthetic phonics – are the best way of teaching children the basic building blocks of reading and writing is now absolutely clear. The Conservatives welcome the Government review of the National Literacy Strategy, but we are clear about the stand that should be taken and the battles that will have to be fought: phonics works. Tiptoeing gently around this subject gets us nowhere. Another review and yet another cohort of children will pass into secondary school unable to read and unprepared to learn. The Government has to say what works clearly, make the change and actually follow it through to the end.

If children do not learn to respect authority at school, how can we expect them to respect others when they grow up? We all know that lack of discipline is an issue that affects most schools, and cripples the learning process in many. The figures bear this out. A teacher is assaulted every seven minutes of the school day. 17,000 pupils were expelled in a single term recently for violent behaviour.

The Government has decided to hold another review. This is perfectly reasonable as long as something comes of it. Yet often with this Government, calling for a review is seen as the end of the process. We want to see the following clear and decisive action: the unambiguous right for heads to expel unruly pupils – so it is clear where authority lies; the abolition of appeals panels – so that heads cannot be undermined by having their decisions publicly reversed and disruptive children returned to the classroom; and the right to make home/school contracts binding, by letting heads refuse to accept children if parents do not sign them.

On discipline, schools should have autonomy. They are, and should be seen clearly as, places where children go to be taught and to learn, not reception centres for all children irrespective of how they behave. As well as this change in approach to the autonomy of schools, we need something more. Listen to children threatened with punishment who say 'I know my rights', and teachers too frightened to deal robustly with poor behaviour, and it is clear what is happening. We are starting to treat teachers like children, and children like adults. That is wrong – and we should say so.

The system for dealing with Special Educational Needs in this country is based on good intentions. The desire to see all children treated with equal love, care and attention is one we all share. The system is now badly in need of reform, however. In some ways, we are in danger of getting the worst of all worlds: at one end, children who are finding it difficult to keep up are being dragged into the SEN bracket, when what they really need is rigorous teaching methods. At the other end, children with profound needs are being starved of resources and inappropriately placed in mainstream schools.

The move towards inclusion was right for many children. No-one wants to turn the clock back to a time when some children were viewed as 'ineducable'. But the pendulum has swung too far. The ideological obsession with holding all children in the same building for school hours, as if mere proximity connotes something profound or productive, has destroyed the education of many of society's most vulnerable individuals.

It is foolish to assume that some of the most challenged and challenging children in Britain can study alongside their mainstream peers with a few hours of extra assistance here and there, or the part time aid of a teaching assistant now and then. They require constant attention from experts in facilities dedicated to their needs. It is expensive and it is painstaking, but it is right. Similarly, it is wrong to close schools for those with moderate disabilities, whose needs fall in the ground between mainstream and severe. Forced into mainstream schools in which they are inevitably left behind, or alternatively into Severe Learning Disabilities schools in which they are never truly pushed to achieve, the plight of children with moderate learning disabilities is extremely troubling.

Children with learning difficulties or disabilities deserve better than to have their real needs waved away because of their totemic status as representatives of social inclusion. These are our children, not guinea pigs in some giant social experiment. In the name of this inclusion agenda, centres of excellence are being torn down. When such expertise is dispersed, it is very difficult to bring it back together.

A teacher is assaulted every seven minutes of the school day. 17,000 pupils were expelled in a single term recently for violent behaviour.

We have set out some very clear steps for the Government to take. Its recently announced 'audit' of special schools must:

- take account of parents' views, which are too often ignored;
- look at the law, which restricts choice and is biased against special schools;
- cover all special schools, in every part of the country;
- include a moratorium on closing special schools, at least until the audit is complete.

Instead, the Government has in fact announced that it will only look at schools for those with the profoundest needs and disabilities. Yet it is the schools for those with moderate needs that are being closed. I have therefore established a Commission for the Conservative Party, to carry out those tasks I have outlined here. The tragedy is that whilst both reviews are taking places, closures will continue.

One of the things that made people sit up and listen to Labour in 1997 was their promise in the introduction to their Manifesto to set children by ability. They knew that this pledge would send parents a message – that New Labour was different. It would not let egalitarian dogma get in the way of raising school standards, and this is something the Conservatives support. The trouble is that Labour has not delivered on this promise, despite recent research by the academic David Jesson confirming what we already knew – that able students do better when they study together. The brightest need to be set with their peers, so they can soar. The struggling need smaller classes with the best teachers so that the difficulty they are having can be properly addressed. The Government never stops talking about 'stretch', but nothing actually happens.

As well as stretching the brightest and helping those that fall behind, we need to keep children switched on to learning. One of the reasons some young people switch off is that they are bored. At fourteen and fifteen they would like to learn more skills, but that is not what is on offer.

This is not just a personal waste, it is a national waste. Just 28% of young people in the UK are qualified to apprentice, skilled craft and technician level, compared with 51% in France and 65% in Germany. If France and Germany are getting vocational education right, why can't we? The Government and much of the educational establishment have proposed the diploma scheme to address this problem. Yet this answer is flawed in that it entails the death, in any meaningful sense, of the A level. You should never try to improve something that is weak – vocational education – by scrapping something that is fundamentally strong – like the A level.

If we are to improve vocational education and end the snobbery that has surrounded it, if we are to keep young people switched on to learning, then we must take some bold steps, such as the following: funding vocational courses from 14; funding vocational centres that match the best available anywhere in the world; and establishing a simple set of vocational qualifications that businesses do not just understand, but actually design.

Each August, GCSE and A level results come out – and the same thing happens. The debate between the 'best results ever' and 'the easiest exams ever' begins. To avoid this demoralising argument, we need to restore faith in our examinations system. There are real problems. Students that failed Maths A level in 1991 would now get a B. With one exam board in 2004, a student could get an A in Maths GCSE with just 45%. There is a simple principle that must be applied. Exams and their results should differentiate clearly between those pupils who excel, those who do well, those who pass and those who fail. There are various ways to achieve this revaluation. For example, A grades could be reserved for a fixed proportion of students, or marks could be published as well as grades. A revaluation must take place, however, so that parents, employers and students can have confidence in the system.

These are the five challenges that I believe need urgent attention. Beyond the specifics, there lies a more general problem at the heart of British education which we might describe as 'a lack of purpose': students being told the questions to their exams four weeks before they sit them, a history curriculum that asks students to wonder how a soldier felt, rather than teaches them about the battles he fought, and an A level paper today found to be almost identical to a CSE paper thirty years ago are just a few examples of this.

We should be frank about this issue. There has been a deep division in the educational establishment for fifty years between those who think that education is about imparting knowledge, and those who think that it is about encouraging children to learn for themselves. Of course, schools should inspire children. When it comes to the basics, however, we should be blunt: teaching is right, and 'discussion facilitation' is wrong. It is common sense that, especially when very young, children should not be left to blunder around in the dark. Rather, they need to be told some basic, essential things. Discipline, respect for others, responsibility – children are not born with restraint: they need to be taught it. Times tables do not leap unbidden into a child's mind: they must be learned, and once learned, as everyone knows, they are learned for life.

Acquiring knowledge and exploring creatively are linked. But creativity, exploration and self-expression can only come after a child has acquired confidence in using the basic tools of communication, language and number. It is a special type of cruelty that denies children access to the keys to learning for fear of stifling their creativity. It is only through a thorough grounding in literacy, being taught to read, that children are given the chance to communicate on terms of equality with others.

The 'learn for yourself' attitude has been indulged far too much, and that has been to the detriment of the education and lives of children for half a century. It is wrong to pretend that children are adults, that they always know what is best for them. Children will not necessarily all want to learn to read or to spell – just as when they are given a choice between chips and pizza or healthy, nutritious food they are more likely to choose what they like, not what is good for them. At its heart, education must be about giving children what is good for them.

I hope that the messages of this essay are proven to be unnecessary. I hope that in the course of this Parliament, the Government addresses the challenges I have identified. If they do, I will support them every step of the way. The important thing is that it is done, not who does it. The Conservative Party must fight for the reforms I have described, because we want every child to have the best start in life, and we want youngsters to make a success of their careers in order to help build a stronger, better Britain.

The failure of state centralism

Greg Clark MP

That Pledge Card has a lot to answer for. In 1997, Labour published a set of simple, cast-iron commitments as to how they would improve public services. It was a brilliant political success. It spoke of can-do government, promising specific results that could not be fudged.

Yet the paradox is that it is, in part, responsible for an approach to government that is failing, and that is resulting in our public services falling short of the service that the public in other countries take for granted.

It brings with it a model of running our public services in which politicians are in charge, and in which, as a result, control must be centralised in Whitehall, not vested in professionals and the people they serve. A model we might call State Centralism.

State Centralism follows from an electoral strategy. If the Government has been elected on a promise to make specific cuts to waiting lists and class sizes, it clearly must achieve them – by all means necessary. Therein lays the problem. What happens when it turns out that the institutions actually responsible for delivery – individual schools and hospitals, and within them head teachers and teachers, doctors and nurses – do not report directly to government ministers?

What if a head teacher wants to invest more in specialist help for literacy or numeracy rather than in smaller classes? What if a consultant physician considers that the order of treatment should be based on his expert assessment of the seriousness of his patients' conditions? The answer is inevitable. Political promises must not be jeopardised by the judgment of professionals. If the problem is that heads and doctors do not report to ministers, the answer was obvious – they should be made to do so. Having made promises, the Government has progressively willed itself the power to make professionals deliver on their behalf.

Of course, this State Centralist approach – of centralised control, with politicians in charge – has been in the DNA of the Labour Party for generations. It was Aneurin Bevan who decreed that the sound of a dropped bedpan in a hospital in Tredegar must reverberate around Whitehall. So it is unsurprising that this approach has gone beyond securing the specific pledges made back in 1997. State Centralism has come to be emblematic of New Labour's approach to government.

State Centralism is implemented through specific policies through which our public services – indeed our public life – has been made to conform. The first of these policies is that of imposing central targets from Whitehall. The second is tying funding to central objectives. The third is over-bureaucratic audit and inspection. The fourth is rigid terms and conditions.

Centrally-imposed targets

State Centralism has been driven by a policy of targets imposed from the top down. Three features of the target regime under Labour deserve mention.

First, the sheer number of targets has grown dramatically. It is difficult to think of any area of policy, however arcane, that has not been subjected to dozens of 'plans', 'strategies', and 'public service agreements', each imposing a raft of targets. Local authorities, for example, have seen a six-fold expansion since 1997 in the number of mandatory plans required to be submitted to central government .

Second, the scope of targets has been extended to govern process as well as outcomes. Instead of identifying key goals to guide the work of service providers, targets now serve to impose a prescriptive template directing the day-to-day work of front-line professionals. In his valedictory speech as Chairman of the British Medical Association, Dr Ian Bogle said that his 'biggest demotivator has been the deprofessionalisation of medicine brought about by protocols, guidelines and government targets'.[40]

Third, targets are now tied to powerful means of enforcing compliance, through applying both rewards and penalties. This

40 Dr Ian Bogle, spe British Medical Assoc Annual Representati Meeting, 30/6/2003

introduces a degree of pressure to achieve arbitrary targets which forces professionals to stray dangerously from prioritising the interests of the citizens they should serve.

Centrally controlled funding

Central control over funding is perhaps the ultimate means by which central government ensures compliance with its demand for how services are run. The degree of that control, across the spectrum of public services and local government, is extraordinary both by historical and international standards.

Britain is unique in its virtual state monopoly over funding of public services. In no other country that we have studied is funding of education and healthcare so dominated by public funds. People are discouraged by the tax system from choosing to pay for these services and those who do are told that they must have nothing to do with state provision. For those who rely on the state to finance the services they receive, ideological barriers heavily constrain the use of public funds to pay for provision outside the public sector.

Rigid central control is just as much a feature of local government finance. Once again, Britain stands out from virtually every other comparable country in the extent of its centralisation. Only in Ireland among OECD countries is a smaller proportion of local spending financed from local taxes.

Since 1997, this central control of finance has increasingly been used to exert managerial control, in a bid to impose the plethora of targets on public service providers. A total of 66 different revenue streams are currently available to a typical comprehensive school. In healthcare, additional resources are tied to the star rating given to each acute trust. In local government, the proportion of local authorities' resources that are ring-fenced has trebled since 1997. In the voluntary sector, prescriptive central funding mechanisms have diverted charities from their missions and local roots, leading them increasingly to resemble public sector organisations.

Bureaucratic audit and inspection

The character of audit and inspection has undergone a profound change since 1997. Mirroring the other drivers of centralisation, it has evolved from providing a broad framework to protect against serious malpractice and offer reliable performance information, into a prescriptive template dictating how services must be run.

Partly this is because the Government's imposition of targets logically needs to be accompanied by structures to enforce compliance with those targets. Similarly, central control of funding requires that central government hold service providers and local authorities accountable for their use of these funds.

Yet inspection regimes have acquired a life of their own. Not only do they reinforce the prescriptive mechanisms of targets and ring fencing. They add their own layers of prescription, in many areas verging into managerial roles. As with targets, inspection regimes are accompanied by powerful enforcement mechanisms. The results of inspections determine entitlement to funds and freedoms. This creates a damaging compliance culture, where service providers have to waste time acquiring expertise in, as one local government officer put it, 'managing inspections'.

National terms and conditions

Another way in which the Government controls the level of public funding for public services is by stipulating the national terms and conditions on which service providers must recruit staff and buy supplies. The most obvious manifestation of these national terms and conditions is the centralisation of terms and conditions for staff. Of course, national pay bargaining is as much the result of pressure over many years from trades unions as it is of deliberate planning by the Government. But Labour so far remains committed to upholding the *status quo* and has chosen this as the moment to bind non-statutory providers of public services into this framework. An announcement in the 2003 Budget that the Government would introduce a greater regional element to public sector pay bargaining has yet to be followed up with significant proposals.

The combination of these four policies which drive State Centralism under Labour is so damaging across the public services for four main reasons.

First, State Centralism undermines local discretion for front-line professionals. State Centralism has robbed front-line professionals of the freedom they need to go about their work.

Teachers have been denied autonomy over classroom discipline by, for instance, the introduction of exclusion appeals panels. Doctors have been subjected to growing numbers of national standards frameworks that impinge on their clinical autonomy and deny them scope to respond to the particular needs of their patients. Another result of this denial of front-line discretion is to limit scope for innovation. State Centralism destroys the natural laboratory of autonomous professionals and institutions developing better solutions to common problems.

Of course, we expect the Government to protect against serious malpractice and uphold a national threshold of minimum acceptable standards. There is also a need for central oversight to provide reliable information that will help citizens choose between different services. But all too often, the 'one size fits all' approach to regulation adopted by this Government has resulted in a 'lowest common denominator' standard of provision across our public services.

Second, State Centralism squanders taxpayers' money on wasteful bureaucracy. Micromanaging the work of front-line public service providers from Whitehall is an enormous task. It requires the creation of a costly bureaucratic machine devoted to ensuring that front-line staff comply with Whitehall's every demand. The Department for Education and Skills, having already loaded teachers with reams of paperwork, recently sought to help matters with three new guides: 'Good Practice in Cutting Bureaucracy 1', 'Good Practice in Cutting Bureaucracy 2', and the essential 'Bureaucracy Cutting Toolkit'.

The situation is no better in local government. Labour's Best Value regime has resulted in a vast paper trail whose cost has not even been counted by Government. Spending by the Audit Commission alone on local government inspectors has increased sixty-fold since 1997.

Third, State Centralism results in unintended consequences. Central prescriptions for services might be well intentioned, but they rarely result in the intended outcome. Critically ill patients are kept waiting for operations so that hospitals can meet their targets by treating the less ill first. The Audit Commission has highlighted the practice of giving sick patients last-minute appointments; if the patient cannot attend at the relevant time, the Government's guidelines permit the waiting time for that patient to be reset. In some hospitals, patients have been kept waiting in ambulance areas, so that they are not classified as waiting in Accident and Emergency departments. This has the consequence of occupying paramedic staff inside hospitals and delaying emergency ambulance services. During the General Election campaign, the Prime Minister was visibly surprised to hear that the target for GP appointments to be 48 hours or less had resulted in it becoming impossible to book appointments for more than 48 hours ahead.

Fourth, State Centralism undermines a sense of local belonging – denying people a sense of ownership over locally provided public services and eroding the wider sense of belonging in local political communities. The 'civic gospel' preached by Joseph Chamberlain and other Birmingham politicians in the nineteenth century is the best-known, but by no means the only illustration of the vitality that used to characterise local politics. In the United States, state and even county government today is a hotbed of local energy. Yet in the UK, even counties with populations larger than some US states have little freedom to innovate.

The Government throws more and more taxpayers' money at our public services. Yet people are seeing little evidence of improvements in their everyday experiences of them. There is no paradox here. It is not surprising that without reforms to bring about decentralisation, pouring extra resources into them brings hardly any benefits. For as long as central government maintains its suffocating grip on local services, there is little prospect of achieving substantially better outcomes. The result is that people will carry on suffering the damaging consequences we have documented across the public services. Waiting lists will remain stubbornly long. Standards in many schools will continue to be poor. Crime will rise and roads will stay congested. Local government will feel powerless to bring about change in failing communities. In different ways, all these blights on our society are ultimately the price we pay for the State Centralism.

It is no longer good enough to claim that State Centralism is needed to secure fairness across the country. Under our increasingly centralist government, the quality of local schools, hospitals, councils and police forces varies wildly from one area to the next. Yet government-imposed uniformity is preventing the innovation at the front line that will deliver better outcomes for everybody.

Government should allow public service professionals the flexibilities to respond to whatever circumstances local people's needs dictate. It means cutting through the waste caused by stubborn central control. And it means enabling front-line staff to drive the innovation that will bring about higher standards for all.

In the Britain of today, the diversity of individual needs and preferences must be matched by just as much diversity in the provision of services.

It does not have to be this way. The last eight years may have seen a steady drift to State Centralism, but it is possible to reverse that process, and free our public services, the professionals who work within them and the citizens who use them from restrictions, targets and central direction. But to do so requires a clear vision of what needs to be achieved in government.

One of the tragic flaws of New Labour is that its precious time in opposition was well spent on reforming the Party and its presentation, but used not at all to think clearly about reforming our public services. So it was inevitable that a tactic of election communication – the pledge card approach – would come to dictate how our public services have been run.

New Labour entered government without a plan for government. And experience shows that if you do not have a clear idea in advance of what you want to achieve, you will never develop one in office. The next Conservative Government needs to be clear about its vision. As far as the public services go, it should be simple.

First, government should do less. The government should not aspire to run things; it certainly should not try to run schools and hospitals from Whitehall. That means every school should be, effectively, an independent school, run by its head and governors. It means every hospital should be an independent hospital. It means repealing the assumption that just because the state pays for a service – like health and education – it has to provide that service.

Just as government should not immerse itself in the detail of running schools and hospitals, neither should it become embroiled in the detail of people's lives. It is a further illustration of the spread of State Centralism that two-thirds of pensioners have to open up their lives to scrutiny by the state in order to claim means-tested benefits. They should have a basic state pension that allows them to live in dignity.

The second element of the approach must be to extend choice. When the Government pays for services it should, wherever possible, fund people to choose, rather than subsidise providers. That is why the right to choose your hospital – from any in the country – is fundamental. Choice drives up standards and stimulates innovation. The same is true in education. Schools should be able to govern themselves and parents should be given the purchasing power the central state currently wields on their behalf.

Sometimes you cannot give choice to individuals. Policing is a good example. In this country at least, you cannot buy your own policeman. But many communities across Britain think they are not getting the type of policing they want – neighbourhood policing, with police officers on the beat. It is entirely possible to give communities more of a say over the type of policing they get. By transferring powers from the Home Office and instead making police forces accountable to local people, it is possible to replace state centralism with greater local accountability.

We must set out policies that will reverse the four drivers of State Centralism that inflict damage across the public services. By reversing these drivers, we can transform public services and government, substituting for the vicious circle of centralisation that exists today a virtuous one of greater local control and choice for citizens. Our aims should be to:

1. Replace central targets with structures better able to respond to the differing needs of individuals and communities:
   a) our priority should be to offer citizens reliable and accessible information about the quality of services;
   b) setting targets should be an independent matter for professional managers themselves, not a political decision.

2. Replace centrally controlled funding with direct funding for citizens and more locally raised finance:
   a) in most cases, money should follow the individual to

wherever they choose to receive services;
b) the distinction between state, voluntary and private providers must be broken down;
c) there should be a better balance between local government spending and local revenue raising, and less central ring-fencing.

3. Replace central audit and inspection with lighter systems of oversight:
a) the role of audit and inspection should primarily be to provide information to help people choose between services, not impose a template on how services are run;
b) of course, there need to be guaranteed minimum standards, but not which hold services back from delivering excellence.

4. Replace national terms and conditions with flexibility to respond to local circumstances:
a) enable service providers to negotiate individually over pay and conditions for their staff;
b) wider local flexibilities to respond to particular market conditions.

The Conservative Government that came to power in 1979 had a mission to reverse the process of state socialism that had reduced the British economy to a state of perpetual crisis. The reforms to the economy implemented in the 1980s have formed the basis for our prosperity in the decades since.

Today, Conservatives face a different challenge. Yet, if we are to reverse the process of State Centralism, the same vigour and certainty of purpose must be applied now as was the case almost thirty years ago.

Labour's State Centralism has failed. People's quality of life is being held back by poor public services and failing communities. Conservatives must explain how giving choice to individual users of public services and real power to local communities will improve public services and reinvigorate local democracy. Only by doing so can we recapture the imagination of the British public and begin a process that will return us to Government.

Women, families and politics: the role of the state

Andrew Lansley CBE MP

At the risk of a lack of humility, I wish to begin by quoting myself. In 2002, I wrote that:

> Labour has a 9% lead over Conservatives among 18-24 year old men, but a 21% lead among 18-24 women. This is despite Labour's loss of student support generally to the Liberal Democrats. Given past Conservative leads over Labour among women voters, we are storing up deep trouble for the Conservative Party if we do not create pro-Conservative sentiments among this age group of young women in the next decade, as they become increasingly settled in long-term voting habits and grow more likely to vote. It is important to recall that, although there is a conventional belief that voters become more Conservative as they become older, it is probably more correct to say that they become conservative, i.e., less willing to change their vote.

At the 2005 General Election, the disconnection between the Conservative Party and younger women voters deepened. Although there was a five-percentage point rise in support for the Conservative Party among men aged 25-34, there was a four-percentage point fall in support among women of the same age.

This is a central issue for the Party. Unless the changes we make substantially increase our support amongst women aged 25–55 at the next General Election, we have no overall prospect of success. Changes important to women voters may unlock other resistant areas of support including those looking to the Conservative Party to offer a more positive alternative.

So why have women increasingly abandoned the Conservative Party at three successive General Elections? Is it because we are a party of men? Of 54 new Conservative MPs, only six are women. Of 197 Conservative MPs, only seventeen are women. Of 354 Labour MPs, 97 are women – four times the proportion. If we had secured 354 seats, fewer than 50 would be women.

When women see the Conservative Party so consistently failing to draw women into its positions of leadership, when they know that the majority of new entrants to some other professions, like medicine and the law, are women, they will ask: do they represent us or understand our problems?

Did we demonstrate that we understood the issues and concerns of women in the last election? Flexible childcare proposals, launched well into the campaign, hardly had time to convince women and younger families that we were serious about balancing work and family life (which always makes it sound easier than it is), and understand the realities of having to make hard, painful decisions about how to maintain family income or whether to be at home with young children.

Further, are younger women voters unwilling to support a party which many of them regard as extreme? When Labour was the party regarded as extreme, the Conservative Party was able to lead from the right. When the Labour Party is seen as camped on the centre ground of politics, right wing policies are characterised as extreme.

By contrast, what do moderate, positive Conservative policies, likely to be attractive to women, look like? They have to start, I think, from an understanding of Britain as it is today. Over the last generation, women's lives in Britain have changed dramatically. More women than ever before now work, with approximately 45% of today's workforce being female.[41] Women are increasingly contributing to business life and to our national economy. Greater numbers of women are using their entrepreneurial skills to set up businesses – 13% of Britain's small businesses are owned by women, and another 43% jointly owned by men and women.[42] While a generation ago fewer than half of Britain's mothers worked, today approximately two thirds do.[43] This means that mothers are increasingly combining work with raising their children; and given the increasing numbers of the very elderly, children are sharing the responsibilities of work with family commitments to care for older relatives. Clearly, the shape of British society is changing.

Despite these changes, we have not witnessed a corresponding change in the dynamics of Britain's decision makers. The risk is that those who represent us nationally or lead us in business and public life will cease to reflect the modern shape of British society. The Conservative Party has particularly suffered from its failure to change.

In the course of the next four years, therefore, we have a challenge. How to convince younger women voters that we share their concerns; that we can offer them positive policies; and can do so in a way which empowers families rather than the state. What should the Conservative Party's programme for women consist of?

First, we must be representative in our Party structures and our elected representations. Parliamentary candidate selection is a key element of this. It is where we are at present least representative. As Theresa May and I recommended four years ago, we must introduce an 'A' list of candidates, drawn up to include candidates who meet testing criteria, but who are more representative than at present. Winnable seats would be required to select from this list unless they had suitable highly qualified local candidates.

Second, we must have an active programme of policy making involving women directly. In the run-up to the 2001 General Election, we published 'Choices', a manifesto for women. In the last Parliament, we did not even have this. In this Parliament, we should do far more. We should have a programme of research and consultation, geared to establishing policies of value to women, understanding women's views on policy options generally, and involving women, including those active in senior positions, in Conservative politics. This programme, while it may be led day-to-day by the Shadow Minister for Women, should be seen as a personal priority for the Leader of the Party.

Third, we must understand the world as it is, not as it used to be. For example, fewer people living in long-term relation-

---

43 Brito, T: *Spousal takes on the mommy Why the Ali Proposal for working mothers*, Duke Journal of Gen and Policy 151.

ships are married; increasing numbers of children are born outside of marriage; increasing numbers of children are growing up in lone parent families; increasingly, mothers of young children are in employment, whether they would prefer to be or not. Our population is getting older; more people are living alone; many are having children later or not at all; and many individuals are relatively isolated from the family support structure of previous generations.

Fourth, we must start with an agenda, of objectives and policy options. Here, the debate on the role of the State in relation to family life, childcare and the work/life balance is crucial. At one end of this debate is the 'get government off our backs' school of thought, which has it that family responsibilities will only be attended to properly by family members and civil society more widely when the state interferes far less than it does today. At the other end of this debate is an approach which seeks to substitute family responsibilities with state provision. Neither is right, nor likely in itself to be effective. We have seen in recent years all too clearly that a lack of family involvement and responsibility has led to serious problems in the progress and discipline of many children. And we can see that state provision fails to secure the emotional engagement which is so essential for young children.

Equally, we can see that many lone parents and disadvantaged families fail to meet their responsibilities without a framework to help them to do so. Our objective must be to create a framework which enables families to maximise their ability for care and support, which offers help to families where they need it, does so in the most accessible way, and intervenes to protect children and the vulnerable where it is essential to do so.

In terms of a policy agenda for this purpose, I suggest a number of options be considered by a new Family Commission on behalf of the Party. These options should include policies put forward before the last election, but which secured insufficient priority and attention, including:

- flexible and enhanced maternity pay;
- flexible child benefit, enabling parents to roll-up child benefit, making it payable not in eighteen years but over three years and at a much higher rate, e.g. £100 a week, to give viable home care options when children are very young;

- tax relief for childcare costs, and flexible childcare payments for low-income families;
- start-up grants for workplace nurseries;
- parenting support through voluntary, faith-based and local commercial organisations, combining support in developing skills with practical, paid-for support in the house for mothers during early months ('doula' style);
- more flexible childminder arrangements under the Working Tax Credit;
- locally based and locally controlled 'Sure Start' arrangements;
- CSA reform, extending simplified formulae to all claims;
- giving all parents options for nursery provision for three-year olds, on a simple voucher basis.

At the heart of this agenda is the idea that parents must be given viable options: to stay at home and look after their children when very young; to return to work and balance work and childcare responsibilities; to choose the nursery and school that is right for their child. It is undeniably an activist agenda. It involves substantial government involvement, so it is essential that it be simple and wherever possible be universal, rather than means-tested. It must also be flexible: allowing parents to design their support rather than having it imposed on them. And it must be led by local government rather than central government, in terms of local structures of provision.

It is a family-centred policy – family meaning in this context those who love and care for children. A further part of this Commission's work would be to consider a similar agenda of care for those looking after family members with disabilities, or the frail and elderly. This agenda should be particularly focused on giving access to direct payment arrangements or control of care budgets, with enhanced respite provision and opportunities to insure against long-term disability through a lifetime savings account with tax advantages.

Importantly, we must recognise that families are not defined by legal status. They are defined by those who love, care for and support others. Family is central to our lives. It is central to a strong society. It is vital that we make government serve families, not override their responsibilities, for it is only through strong families that a strong society will be sustained.

Principles of a Conservative economic policy

George Osborne MP

In my office hangs a set of political cartoons on the walls. Most of the cartoons are 30 years old, satirising a different age in British politics where the political debate was centred on economic policy. One shows Harold Wilson unveiling a car show room called 'Austerity'. Another depicts Dennis Healey in a balloon called 'Hyper Inflation' trying to avoid a mountain called 'Unemployment'. The most telling has the three party leaders at the time – Wilson, Heath and Thorpe – clutching their manifestos as they are engulfed by an avalanche called 'Inflation'.

We do not see many political cartoons like these in the papers today – in large part due to economic reforms brought about by eighteen years of Conservative government. However, these cartoons remind us of one of our core beliefs: that a strong society depends on a strong economy, for without a strong and stable economy, politicians are unable to deliver change in social policy.

Conservatives need to remember that we still lag a long way behind the Labour Party when it comes to public confidence in our ability to manage the economy. However interesting our social policies may be, we will not have the chance to implement them until we gain public confidence in our economic policies. I believe we regain this credibility by setting out a long-term vision for Britain's economic success. This lies in four economic principles: macroeconomic stability; increased productivity; reduced long-term demands on the state; and lower taxes.

Before the 1970s, the prevailing wisdom was to use microeconomic policy to target inflation – through the prices and incomes policies – and to use macroeconomic policy to target growth, by using monetary and fiscal policy in a number of aborted attempts to 'dash for growth'.

By the late 1970s, it was clear that this approach had failed. The architects of Conservative economic policy realised that we had to perform an about-turn in economic strategy. Microeconomic policies were used to target unemployment and underlying trend growth, and macroeconomic policies were used to target inflation. That change, most eloquently set out by Nigel Lawson in a landmark lecture in 1984, represented a one hundred and eighty degree reversal of previous policy.

In our microeconomic, supply side reforms, we were enormously successful. We had a broad economic policy that: freed us from exchange and price controls; challenged the militancy of trades unions; enhanced competition; privatised swathes of unproductive industry; and reformed the labour market so that firms were freer to create jobs and prosperity.

Our macroeconomic policy brought more success to the job of beating inflation. We developed a series of monetary policy tools to fight inflation – first monetary targeting, then exchange rate targeting, and the exchange rate mechanism. But it was only after the exit from the ERM in 1992 that the best tool came to the fore: inflation targeting. Before then, inflation targeting was an idea whose time had not yet come.

It is a supreme irony that the moment the Conservative Party lost the trust of the electorate on economic matters was the moment that we implemented the most successful macroeconomic strategy in modern times. Inflation targeting since 1992 has so far delivered 52 quarters of uninterrupted economic growth, low inflation, and gradually falling unemployment – the first nineteen of which, I constantly have to remind the Chancellor, happened under a Conservative government.

What lessons did Labour take from this? It took them over a decade to come to terms with the changes brought about by those great reforming Conservative governments. But by the mid 1990s, Tony Blair and Gordon Brown at last came to terms with the Thatcher revolution. They pledged to stick to Conservative spending plans, promised not to raise income tax rates, and accepted that the main trades unions reforms and privatisations were irreversible. Establishing economic credibility allowed them to persuade the public that they could then deliver on their other promises of social justice. Economic efficiency and social justice looked plausible. They went from the politics of 'or' to the politics of 'and'.

Now, after what will be at least twelve years of a Labour Government, we too have to come to terms with the changes that have happened. In economic policy, Labour immediately made the Bank of England independent and gave it a symmetric inflation target. They formalised the principles that by then governed Conservative fiscal policy, and communicated them in two bite-sized rules: the 'golden rule' and the 'sustainable investment rule'. In other words, they took the next steps in the building on the successful economic framework they inherited from the Conservatives. This framework now needs revitalising to make it credible again.

We must recognise that these developments have improved the macroeconomic management of the UK economy. And I believe that we should support the Government when they advocate policies that are right for the country; for too often we have been perceived as opportunistic. Although we laid the foundation for the macroeconomic stability that Britain has enjoyed, we lost credit for it by voting against the Bank of England's independence. We have talked about reform of public services, but we voted against the creation of foundation hospitals. We have made theoretical arguments in favour of a smaller state, but in practice, we voted against tuition fees. We have consistently opposed strikes yet tacitly supported the fuel protestors who brought England to a virtual stand still.

Too often, we have sacrificed long-term credibility for the prospect of winning the support of an aggrieved section of the population or the possibility of winning a vote in the House of Commons. Our short-termism has hampered attempts to develop a long-term economic policy.

I am not looking for any scapegoats. As someone involved in the Opposition since 1997 I blame myself as much as anyone else. But I have learnt my lesson, and I would urge my colleagues not to fall into the same trap this Parliament. We must never again confuse populism with popularity. As we acknowledge that some of the Government's policies have been good for the economy and the country, Conservatives gain credibility to criticise Labour in the areas where they have made real mistakes – of which there have been plenty.

Gordon Brown's success on macroeconomic policy has obscured a microeconomic policy that has been damaging to the functioning of the economy in the long run. The CBI estimate that taxes on business have risen by £43 billion since 1997. Sir David Arculus estimates that the cost of regulation is now a staggering £150 billion, of which one third is administration costs. The Chancellor interferes with business, not through ownership as Labour once did, but through intrusive regulation.

The Chancellor has extended a dependency culture and increased the long-term demands placed on the state. The slice of national spending made by the state has risen from 37% to 41%. The long-term effects are apparent: our productivity growth rate has fallen to half that of the United States – and recently fell again, and Britain has fallen from 4th to 11th in the world competitiveness league table.

Certainly, Gordon Brown has not been the worst Chancellor that this country has ever seen. We have had twelve years of growth, low inflation and falling unemployment. But he is being wasteful, has raised taxes, over-regulates, and meddles. He has fiddled his own fiscal rules and so thrown out his credibility. This is exactly the opposite of what Britain needs to do to compete in the modern world.

China now produces two million graduates a year, India has 1300 engineering colleges. It costs eight times more to train an engineer in Britain as it does in Slovakia.[44] In the past, we only faced international competition for our low-skilled jobs, yet now our high skill, high paid jobs are at risk as well. Unfortunately, Gordon Brown is failing to meet the economic challenges posed by globalisation; his microeconomic policies are taking us in the wrong direction. So the Opposition needs to lay before the country a broad, credible economic policy: one with the over-arching ambition to achieve rising living standards in the midst of the 21st century global economy.

In a fiercely competitive world where businesses, wealth creators and capital can move almost anywhere, Britain cannot afford to be second best. We need an economic policy that pro-

44 See "Principles Conservative econor policy", 5 July 2005 http://www.cps.org.u 61.doc

vides stability, improves the productivity of our workforce, makes the state both efficient and effective with taxpayers' money, and reduces long-term demands on the taxpayer. I believe that there should be four objectives of Conservative economic policy, as follows.

Reinforce macroeconomic stability: Economic stability cannot be guaranteed by the government. But bad government policy can guarantee economic instability. We must always be fiscally responsible – unlike the current Chancellor, who has fiddled his economic cycle to cheat on the golden rule. He has a structural deficit; he is coming up against the ceiling of his sustainable investment rule; and the economy is growing below trend.

Instead, we should be strengthening macroeconomic stability. Not only by ensuring the Bank of England's independence, but also by establishing an independent National Statistical Service to bring confidence back to government data. The Chancellor has refused to include PFI liabilities as government debt; this a clear affront to the transparency of his sustainable investment rules.

We should establish independence in fiscal forecasts through a Fiscal Projections Committee that will give real force to the golden rule. In opposition, Gordon Brown thought this was a good idea. In 1995, he called for a 'panel of independent forecasters' to judge the golden rule. Once in government, however, he ditched the idea and now has changed the fiscal goal posts in the middle of the game. We need an independent referee to make sure there is no more cheating.

Increase the productivity of the economy: Gordon Brown was right when he said that 'productivity is a fundamental yardstick of economic performance'. Only by constantly adding value can we hope to compete against economies where wages are lower. Productivity growth is the only way to improve competitiveness without cutting wages.

The Chancellor's excessive regulation and higher taxes have stalled Britain's productivity growth at just 1.3% – down from an average of 2.1% over the last eight years under the Conservatives. By contrast, America's productivity growth has increased and is now more than double ours.

Conservatives can ameliorate poor productivity by tackling regulation and business taxes, improving the skills of our workforce, and encouraging technological progress and scientific advance.

Tackling the growth of the public sector is also a crucial part of improving productivity, for it crowds out the rest of the economy. Public sector employment has risen by over half a million. Those people are no longer available to work in the private sector, inhibiting businesses' ability to grow. In some parts of the country, like the North East and the Midlands, private sector employment has actually fallen under Labour.

In an age of unprecedented international competition, and with a stable macroeconomic background, businesses cannot bid up the price of these resources, as it used to, in an inflationary spiral. Instead, we miss opportunities to expand productive capacity and create wealth. So unless those skills in the public sector are freed up, the economy counts the cost, economically and socially. That is why public service reform is critical to remain competitive.

One aspect of reform is to examine ways to include the private sector in delivering services. I reject absolutely Labour's view that there should be a state monopoly in providing health care and schooling. It is important that health and education are publicly funded and free at the point of use, but that does not mean every doctor, teacher and nurse needs to be employed by the state.

Gordon Brown has been the roadblock to reform in this Government. But where a little diversity of provision has been forced upon the Chancellor, such as NHS Treatment Centres, we are already seeing the benefits with big increases in productivity. However, as Conservatives, we can go much further than Brown or Blair; we view public service reforms as a means to improve delivery, achieve productivity, and generate growth throughout the whole economy.

Reduce the long-term demands on the state: Sometimes in our discourse concerning the role of the state, Conservatives have tended to sound as if we are limited in our aspirations for government; as if we think that government is so much a part of the problem that it cannot really offer any positive solutions.

I believe it is right that government should ensure all children have access to an excellent school, provide everyone with access to first class health care, and help families with childcare.

The government can and should provide a safety net below which none can fall. Yet we cannot be satisfied with a situation where the public sector takes an ever-increasing share of our national income. It damages economic dynamism and undermines the civic society that underpins our freedom.

The James Report was a powerful indictment of government waste, and we were right to look for ways to improve the efficiency of government: reduce the headcount of the civil service and rationalise the plethora of government quangos. But it was not enough. Politicians always talk about reducing bureaucracy and red tape. Conservatives need to make a number of significant, real and credible reductions in the long-term demands on the state. That way, we can concentrate valuable resources on those who really need them.

We should start by taking a long, hard look at Gordon Brown's tax credit system. The administrative chaos and ministerial mismanagement involved in this failure has plunged thousands of families into hardship and cost the taxpayer billions of pounds. Conservatives believe in helping people in low-paid jobs, because that assistance moves many from welfare to work – which is why we introduced the Family Credit. Yet we should ask ourselves whether taxpayers earning incomes of £15,000 should really be providing means-tested income support to people earning up to £66,000 a year.

Another area where we should consider reducing future demand on the state is public sector pensions. This huge government liability, currently estimated to cost between £500bn and £690bn,[45] lies hidden from the Government's books. At a time when life expectancy has increased and when millions of people in the private sector have seen their pensions reduced and their final salary schemes closed, how can we justify making them pay taxes to support generous, unfunded public sector pensions. Is it right that many civil servants contribute 3.5% of their salary to their pensions when most people are being asked to contribute at least 6%?

The Government proposed public sector pension reform last autumn and then backtracked in the face of opposition from their public sector union paymasters. We should show more resolve.

We desperately need to update Britain's crumbling transport infrastructure. And in the case of roads, we can do that by paying for new roads through tolling. The toll road around Birmingham has been an enormous success, decreasing journey times both for those who pay on the new road, and for those who stick to the old. And it was built without increasing the burden on the taxpayer at all. Instead, it was built on the principle that those who use it pay.

By reducing long-term demands on the state, we can reverse the ever-increasing taxes that must inevitably follow inefficient big-government programs.

Lower taxes: The Conservative Party has always, correctly, put forward the case for lower taxes, but often has failed to set that in the context of a broader economic strategy. We must show how lower taxes support our wider economic objectives.

I saw in Estonia how a low and simple tax system helps individuals and businesses. Simpler taxes save everyone time and money. They remove the need for people to waste their lives trying to find loopholes, and for others to have to plug them. Britain's economy would be more productive if those involved in the war of attrition between tax planners and taxmen spent their lives building businesses and creating jobs.

To compete in the increasingly competitive global environment, where businesses and skilled individuals can 'vote with their feet', simplicity is not enough. We need lower taxes – particularly lower business taxes. Most developed countries are cutting their business tax rates in order to compete with the emerging economies in Asia and the flat tax systems of New

---

We need lower taxes – particularly lower business taxes. Most developed countries are cutting their business tax rates in order to compete with the emerging economies in Asia and the flat tax systems of New Europe.

Europe. The United States has cut taxes on dividends and investment. Germany is planning to cut its federal corporate tax rates. Ireland has pioneered low business taxes and reaped the reward in foreign direct investment. However, Britain is being left behind. Far from looking at ways to reduce taxes, independent experts believe that the Chancellor will almost certainly have to raise them to pay for his fiscal mismanagement. The problem is that the global economy will no longer tolerate high tax systems of the kind that Gordon Brown is building.

Conservatives need to strike out in a different direction. In explaining how our economic policy will create long-term growth and prosperity, we should consistently advocate simpler and lower taxes from the beginning of this Parliament right until the next polling day.

The four principles of the Conservative economic policy – macroeconomic stability, increased productivity, reduced demand on the state, and lower taxes – allow us to communicate a vision to the public about how Britain can continue to create wealth through the private sector, provide security through public service reform, and raise living standards in an increasingly competitive and mobile business market.

The foundation of a strong society is a strong economy. We need to establish our credibility with the public as people who can be trusted to run the economy, and we must show how we are better placed than our opponents to meet the challenges of globalisation and capitalise on the opportunities of these new emerging economies. But to do that we should never sacrifice long-term credibility for short-term opportunity.

Love, money and time: how to grow civil society

Danny Kruger

There is, Oliver Letwin once wrote in a book for the Social Market Foundation, 'a tension which stubbornly persists in our politics'. The tension is within each of us, between 'our anger at constriction and our dread of loneliness'; between the desire to be free and the desire to belong.

Philosophers have found many ways to categorise this tension. Among the most familiar are Michael Oakeshott's 'civil state' and 'enterprise state'; Isaiah Berlin's 'negative liberty' and 'positive liberty'; Ferdinand Tonnies' *Gemeinschaft* and *Gesellschaft*; and Jonathan Sacks' *mishpat* and *tzedekah*. All describe the difference between a system of strict individual freedom and a state of warm social membership. In our politics, the tension is in the difference between Whigs (or liberals) and Tories (or conservatives); between Edmund Burke's love of the American Revolution and his hatred of the French Revolution; and between Adam Smith's *Wealth of Nations* and his *Theory of Moral Sentiments*.

These two strands of the centre-right tradition – freedom and belonging – have different spheres. One exists in the sphere of law and rights – what used to be called 'civil rights' – which is to say, in the sphere of the state. The other exists in the sphere of society: the multitudinous memberships, habits and affiliations that give us our local and particular identity. Many of the problems of our politics lie in the confusion of these two spheres. Indeed, the essential trick of the left is to conflate the two distinct principles – freedom and belonging; to confuse the personal autonomy guaranteed by the state with the identity we gain through our social membership. Hence, in particular, the contradictions of the political doctrine of multiculturalism. On the one hand, we attempt to hold fast to the traditional Lockean idea of the state as existing to preserve our liberty and our equality before the law. On the other hand, we have decided that the state must also recognise, preserve and even 'celebrate' our distinct social identities. And the latter idea is winning out: rather than attempting to be 'colour-blind', for instance, the government focuses on 'diversity'.[46]

In the same way, the state has assumed responsibility for managing, even owning, the institutions that cater to communal needs. The nationalisation of education, healthcare, welfare and pensions were all steps in the process by which the agency of freedom – the state – transmuted into the agency of belonging. The category error is apparent in the fact that these nationalisations, to varying degrees and in various ways, have proved a failure, eroding freedom without promoting belonging.

If the error of the left is a soft-minded conflation of two distinct principles – freedom and belonging – the error of the modern right is often a hard-hearted indifference to one of them: belonging. We are loud in defence of individual freedom and civil liberties: we tend to regard as weak or 'wet' a concern for the social identities and cultures which give meaning to life. Much of the dismay that the electorate has towards the Conservative Party, I suspect, is due to the widespread sense that we are – in the phrase heard by David Willetts on the doorstep during the 1992 election – the 'wrecking crew'. During the 1980s, much was done to liberate the individual from the bondage of state industry and the closed shop. Yet this was achieved at the price of much dismantling: labour mobility put strain on families; competition broke up large, stable monopolies; and economies of scale forced small businesses to close.

To summarise: there is an ancient and inherent tension in our culture between freedom and belonging. During the 1980s, the right privileged freedom over belonging. The left's response has been to deploy the state in the service of belonging, which is an artificial and damaging thing to do, inimical to both freedom and belonging. The right's response must not be cravenly to follow suit, in an attempt at public repentance. Nor must it be to repeat earlier mistakes, and dismiss all talk of belonging as a Trojan horse for more state control. There is a third way.

* * *

Letwin says the 'stubborn tension' between freedom and belonging cannot be 'theorised away'. Indeed, it cannot. It can however be accommodated: demilitarised, as it were, and made fruitful. The solution is to be found in civil society.

Civil society, as Matthew Spalding of the Heritage Foundation in Washington D.C. explains, is valuable precisely because it performs the job which the left takes to be the job of the state:

> The traditional associations of civil society – families, schools, churches, voluntary organisations, and other mediating institutions – sustain social order and public morality, moderate individualism and materialism, and cultivate the personal character that is the foundation of a self-governing society. All of this occurs without the aid of government bureaucracies or the coercive power of the law.[47]

Francis Fukuyama has said that the premise of his seminal book *The End of History* does not apply to civil society. Whereas at the economic and political level, debate in the rich world has largely ceased, at the level of society and culture controversy still rages. Fukuyama agrees with his great antagonist Samuel Huntingdon that, as he puts it, 'the chief issue in world politics henceforth will be the cultural issue'. Hence his next book, *Trust*, which was an attempt to identify the cultural and social habits which underpin political and economic models. He argues that low-trust societies, where 'the art of association is attenuated' (he cites China, Italy and France as examples) are those in which a 'very centralised bureaucratic state' has had 'ambitions to take as much of civil society under its wing as possible'.

This insight – that the large state is inimical to a healthy society – is fundamental to conservatism. We object to the large state not merely because it erodes individual freedom: worse, it damages the social fabric and limits the capacity of the economy. The left do not see things that way, of course. Anthony Giddens, the doyen of the intellectual left, believes that markets depend

[47] Spalding, M: *Prin... and Reforms for Citiz... Service*, Heritage Fou... 1 April 2003.

on 'a social and ethical framework – which they themselves cannot provide', and that therefore 'ethical standards' have to be brought in from outside – from a public ethics, guaranteed in law'. Conservatives disagree. The 'social and economic framework' for markets is not provided by 'public ethics, guaranteed in law' (i.e. by the state) but by private ethics, immanent in the culture (i.e. by society).

The left regard society as the ally – indeed the subsidiary – of the state, in a 'partnership' against markets: as Professor Giddens puts it, 'government and communities' must together correct the failings of 'the market'. The right disagrees: markets and communities must together correct the failings of the state.

The consanguinity of society and the market – of community and the individual – is a staple of the Anglo-Saxon political tradition. Fukuyama quotes Max Weber, visiting America at the end of the 19th century and finding to his surprise that freedom has generated order:

> You would think that the United States, given the individualism embedded in its constitution, should resemble a formless heap of sand, but in fact it has this lumpy quality where the grains of sand adhere to one another.[48]

Though Anglo-Saxons tend to stress the concept most, in fact it was another German, Hegel, who first emphasised the role of civil society. He did so in a way that demonstrated the closeness of freedom and social life. Following Karl Popper's hostile account of him in *The Open Society and its Enemies*, Hegel is often caricatured as a statist; a proto-fascist who wished to subsume the individual in the state. In fact, he explicitly argued for a separate civil sphere between the individual and the government, merely arguing that the individual is, paradoxically, most 'free' when he is enfolded in the embrace of others. It is a sad reflection on liberals of Popper's stamp that, by associating the advocates of civil society with the advocates of statism, they unwittingly do the job of the left.

Hegel's anti-statism is apparent in his definition of civil society. He did not, as many do, distinguish between the 'profit' and 'non-profit' sectors. Civil society, to Hegel, included the commercial marketplace. It rarely does so today: civil society is taken to mean the non-profit sector, and many of its advocates (including romantic anti-capitalist Tories) celebrate this quality. This is an intellectual lapse. For though there is a large role to be played by the voluntary sector in the delivery of public services and the regeneration of communities, we should not connive, even implicitly, in the demonisation of profit.

Even the most 'altruistic' medical and academic professionals, those most thoroughly imbued with the public service ethos, exist in the commercial world: they offer their labour in exchange for money, and bleat loudly when they are not paid what they think they are due. What is a doctor's salary but his 'profit', paid by the taxpayer; does not a teacher profit from education – are not his holidays in Spain a scandalous diversion of public funds for private fun? Meanwhile, on the other side of the equation, is a corner shop or a pub primarily a commercial or a social institution? Is a family-run private preparatory school run for profit or because the owners are committed to education?

It is by reclaiming the commercial sector for civil society that we can best make the moral case for capitalism, as the generator not only of financial capital but of social capital too. And it will allow us to understand the voluntary sector in a new way: not as an offshoot of government, sharing the 'ethos' (and often exchanging the personnel) of the state bureaucracy; but as a dynamic, innovative organism which contains within it the germ of its own growth.

170 years ago, Alexis de Tocqueville distinguished French, British and American society thus: in France, social action was a function of the state; in Britain, it was a function of the aristocracy and gentry; in America, it was a function of voluntary associations. While the American model was best, said de Tocqueville, the British was superior to the French. For while in France the aristocracy was effectively subsumed in the state, bound together in the *ancien regime*, in Britain the aristocracy maintained a proud separation from the Queen's government. There was, therefore, the opportunity for social action managed by local agents independent of the state. And as the locus of power shifted down the social hierarchy, the American, or voluntary, model came to supplant the aristocratic one. One of the first such organisations, the Hearts of Oak Benefit Society, set out the basic principle as early as 1842 in the preface to its

rules of membership:

> Providence has given no man an indemnity from affliction, disease and death; it is a duty, therefore, that every man owes himself and his family, to provide against these exigencies and that distress which invariably attends their visitations.[49]

By the end of the nineteenth century, although a considerable proportion of British social action remained the preserve of paternalist philanthropy, there had been a significant rise in self-help and mutual aid. Britain was becoming more like America. In the twentieth century, however, first under the influence of Lloyd George's Liberal Party (especially the 'fateful decision' of 1911, as Beveridge later described it, to use existing friendly societies to administer a state benefit) and then under that of Attlee's Labour Party, Britain became steadily more like France.

A new aristocracy has arisen, and the *nouveau regime* in Britain looks rather like the *ancien regime* in France. A class of enlightened grandees, nominally independent of the government but in reality fully subservient to it, now manages huge swathes of public life, entirely unaccountable to local communities and accountable to the nation as a whole only via the attenuated link between ministers and Parliament. Meanwhile, once-proud independent bodies, most notably trades unions (which began life in the eighteenth and nineteenth centuries as underground organisations compelled by government proscription to keep their distance from the state), have become mere public advocates for more central control. Trades unions now serve their members not – as formerly – by providing them with healthcare, pensions and other benefits, but by lobbying Whitehall for higher taxes, higher public spending and greater government control over civic institutions.

A further depressing development began with an admirable reform introduced by the Conservatives: contracting-out. Civil society organisations – including, very properly, commercial businesses – acquired the responsibility for running public sector institutions under contract to the government. While much progress was achieved under contracting-out and its descendants, such as the Private Finance Initiative, the overall effect has not been to 'socialise' the state, but to 'statify' society. The left's analysis – that government and civil society are partners – has been realised.

The problem is more acute in America, where more has been done to contract with private providers. Stanley Carlson-Thies, who resigned from President Bush's Office of Faith-Based and Community Initiatives in 2002, explained why: 'the key aim [became] to persuade more faith-based groups to partner with government, rather than to persuade the government to become more hospitable to faith-based groups'.

Carlson-Thies was talking specifically about the tendency of government to require religious organisations to dilute their religious ethos in order to qualify for public money, but the problem applies in the secular sphere, too. 'Partnering' the state with civil society is invariably destructive of the latter, unless real safeguards are built in. The planners of Lyndon Johnson's Great Society in the 1960s deliberately contracted with private providers in order to build political support. As Smith and Lipsky point out in their book *Non-Profits for Hire: the welfare state in the age of contracting*, the result has not been positive:

> Instead of shrinking the role of government and making the provision of public services subject to market discipline, contracting has actually diminished and constrained the community sector by government intervention in non-profit organisations.[50]

Schools, hospitals and welfare agencies are all properly institutions of civil society, not of the state. They are (or should be) private agencies, staffed by private agents. They may be licensed by the government to fulfil nationally decreed functions in exchange for taxpayers' money, but they should be independently owned and managed, and accountable for their performance to their users and the local community. We must ensure, as Beveridge put it, that in seeking 'co-operation between public and voluntary agencies', the voluntary agency 'has a will and life of its own'.

If the tension between freedom and belonging is '*the* problem of our times', as Letwin says, *the* challenge of our politics is the battle for civil society. And we see the delusive appeal of the left most acutely here. For the left can claim to support civil society because its preferred agency – the state – directly assists

50 Smith and Lipsky, *Profits for Hire: the welfare state in the age of contracting*. Harvard University, 1993.

the institutions which make it up. They fund schools and hospitals through direct public subsidy, or block grants. The right, meanwhile, lets individuals make their own choices of how to spend their own money – or, when state funding is deemed appropriate, does so through voucher schemes. In short, we let institutions shift for themselves. Our policy, therefore, is open to the charge of being individualistic, even 'atomistic'; we are seen to have little concern for the associations and institutions which bind individuals together.

The challenge for the right, then, is convincingly to show that the interests of institutions are best served by a policy of individual choice. We must argue that state funding of institutions is detrimental to them, because it removes the independence and innovation which makes them effective. And we must argue that a policy of individual choice, by making institutions directly accountable to the people they serve, not only makes them more responsive to their users, but also ties their users' affections to them. A relationship is established by the free decision of the individual to engage with the independent provider of a service; rather than being mediated, and thereby disrupted, by the state, the relationship becomes reciprocal and enduring.

The main obstacle to such a change is, perversely, civil society institutions themselves, which in many cases have been corrupted by the left's analysis. The people who run our large institutions – and the institutions which serve them, in local government and the quangos – are themselves imbued with the notion that their interests are best served by 'partnership' with government. Naturally enough, they want to have their cake and eat it: they resent government's interference in their activities, but they do not want to lose the intravenous drip represented by state funding. They want to be independent, but block-funded. That is, they want to be accountable to no-one.

This cannot be. An institution, no less than an individual, cannot exist isolated from others – every school and hospital, welfare agency and care home must be accountable somewhere. What we need to persuade people of is that institutions should be accountable downwards and outwards, to the people they serve, not upwards to the government.

How do we achieve such a situation, where individuals

and institutions are free to relate to each other naturally and spontaneously? One answer is the libertarian one: government should withdraw altogether from the social sphere, returning to its limited, Lockean role as the guarantor of our equality under the rule of law. People would then be free to apply their own money – which would be taxed only minutely in order to enforce the law – to the institutions which, free of government regulation, would spring up to serve them.

This is, of course, the basic paradigm of the liberal-conservative position. There is a problem, however, described in the 'I wouldn't start from here' argument. Just as the example of Russia after 1990 shows, when a large state has so effectively destroyed the institutions of freedom, *laisser-faire* leads not to their regeneration, but to an oligopoly which is itself inimical to civil society. As Fukuyama says, 'getting government out of the way is only half the story':

> There is a certain assumption [among conservatives] that civil society, once having been damaged by the excessive ambition of government, will simply spring back to life like brine shrimp that have been freeze-dried, and now you add water to them and they become shrimp again. It is not something that you can necessarily take for granted.[51]

In one sense, government's first priority is indeed to get out of the way. In particular, this means ending the system by which civil society organisations are forced to compete on unfair terms with public agencies. Indeed the essential incompatibility of the state and society – the fallacious partnership – is apparent in the unfair competition between them. Many charities complain about the discrimination they face when bidding against public sector agencies for public sector contracts; even commercial operators have an advantage in that they are allowed to claim back their overheads, which social enterprises are not.

To achieve a level playing field a radical step must be taken: a single regulatory system for public and private providers, and an anti-discrimination clause in all bidding contracts. As under 'charitable choice' law in the United States, the precise legal status or the particular ethic of a provider should have no bearing on its application for a publicly funded job:

---

51 Fukuyama, F: Th Association Social Ca the Global Economy, November 13, 1995

the only consideration should be its effectiveness.

To realise this system will require another major step. For the danger of a single regulatory framework is what Joseph Leconte of the Heritage Institute calls 'the fatal embrace': such a system could easily become the means by which independent organisations are dragged into the net of the state. The traffic must be in the opposite direction: we need a comprehensive transfer of assets, so that all state-owned organisations currently active in the social sphere acquire a new 'social' status, whether as charities, trusts, or companies limited by guarantee. Asset transfer will, of course, require a restrictive covenant that the asset will continue to be used for public purposes. And in many cases, where individual choice through a voucher is not appropriate – such as the management of public parks or libraries – the transfer might also include an endowment or a regular income stream from public funds.

Asset transfer is a precondition, not the conclusion of the process of restoring civil society. There are three policy areas which – though they too involve a smaller state – require real political leadership. These can be categorised as: promoting faith-based social action; stimulating a culture of private giving; and stimulating a culture of volunteering. Or put another way: love, money and time.

Fukuyama believes that the 'lumpy quality' of American life identified by Weber, the tendency of individuals 'to adhere to one another', is attributable to its history of religious pluralism. The associative spirit first noticed by de Tocqueville has always found its expression in churches, since the days when dissenting exiles from Britain found sanctuary in the New World. When religious toleration was enacted in Britain in the nineteenth century, the dissenting tradition became a powerful social agent here too. Cities like Birmingham grew up around the churches and chapels of Methodists and Baptists, Quakers and Congregationalists, which all regarded it as a duty of their faith to be actively involved with the improvement not only of morals and manners, but also of the living conditions of their fellow citizens.

Today, we can take inspiration, as modern Americans have, from this history. The virtue of faith-based social action is that it comes with *love* – the word which modern translations of 1

Corinthians 13 ('the greatest of these is...') have substituted for King James' 'charity'. Inspired by religion, charity is not a grim duty, nor the expiation of guilt, nor the mechanical pursuit of Marxist equality, but an act of devotion. Christians see Christ in those who suffer ('what you do to the least of these, you do to Me') and the other faiths also stress the moral imperative of compassion. As studies in every area of social action – particularly in such intractable challenges as the rehabilitation of prisoners and drug addicts – have shown, faith-based action is supremely effective.

Britain has an advantage and a disadvantage over America in this area. The advantage is political: there is no constitutional bar on faith-based activity in the public sphere. The disadvantage is social: there is far less faith-based capacity here. While America is the most church-going society in the western world, Britain is the least (54% of Americans go to church once a month, compared to 20% of Britons).[52]

The advantage and disadvantage are apparent in the large number of 'church schools' in Britain (unthinkable in the US) which yet behave and are regarded as almost entirely secular institutions. Therefore, though non-discrimination legislation, as described above, is necessary, our main need is not a 'faith-based initiative' on the George W. Bush model, i.e. a plan to pull down barriers to church involvement in welfare. What we need is concerted and deliberate action to foster new faith-based organisations and to fund them with taxpayers' money.

The argument is sometimes made that public money should not be spent on religious organisations – that religion is a private thing and therefore disqualified from public funding. But this argument is intellectually weak, for it rests on the supposition that a service provider, any less than an individual, can be philosophically and morally null. We all bring our morals and our world-view to bear on our work, and the work of social activists in particular – involved in education and healthcare, welfare and care for the elderly, punishment and rehabilitation – is acutely moral.

An atheist is not morally neutral, not devoid of assumptions about human nature and human capability; atheism too is a faith position, albeit a young, Western and tiny one when seen in the context of history and the rest of the world. To exclude

---

52 See Church Serv. Attendance Statistic. the Barna Group, http://www.barna.org e.aspx?Page=Topic& =10

from social action organisations proclaiming theist worldviews, and admit only those of a minority faith of recent and local growth, is hardly liberal or enlightened.

In the one regard where the anxiety about faith-based organisations is valid, the anxiety is catered for. It is reasonable to expect organisations not to use public money for the purpose of proselytising, especially when the client of the service has no choice over where to receive it. When he has a choice, of course – by means of a voucher – there can be no objection; if he does not like the hymns he can leave. But when the funding comes from above and the client is allocated to a provider – as must happen in some cases, for instance mental health care – it is right to avoid publicly-funded evangelism.

Here too, there is a way round the problem. American 'charitable choice' law (which makes it illegal for federal grant-makers to exclude organisations for funding because of their religious belief) specifically erects a Chinese wall between the organisation's secular/welfare functions and its religious/evangelist functions – the latter must be privately funded and organisationally separate from the former. Of course, the Chinese wall is a difficult one to police. And yet, for all the overlap, aggressive secularists need not worry. As Robert Wuthnow, in his critical book *Saving America? Faith-based services and the future of civil society*, points out, most faith-based organisations are not as religious as all that: 'the most valuable asset of church-based charities is that they foster social relationships, not that they inculcate religious ideals'.[53]

The second area of policy is money. And it is money that most clearly shows the annexation of civil society by the state. In Britain, charities receive more of their income from the government than from private citizens; in America, it is the other way around. Yet for all the democratic mandate of the government, the British model is hardly popular. A recent survey for the Centre for Social Justice showed that, given £200 to spend on poverty-fighting, no-one – 0% – would choose to give it to the government. They would give it direct to charity.[54]

Levels of philanthropy in the UK are less than half those of the US (around 0.7% of GDP compared to around 2%).[55] One reason which explains this difference is that Americans tend to give to organisations in their community: charity begins at home. Britons, by contrast, give remotely, to large national and international organisations. Indeed, international aid gets the largest piece of the charitable pound.

This suggests to Karen Wright, of the LSE's Centre for Civil Society, a paradigmatic difference in the psychology of giving in the two countries. Americans give 'generously':

> US giving is heavily laced with self-interest, either directly through tax benefits, benefits from the supported charity, or social status... Moral motivation rests on values of individual initiative and reciprocity.

Britons give 'altruistically':

> The British expect that giving should be altruistic, even self-sacrificing... Giving is seen largely as a private decision, and peripheral to both social identity and civic responsibility... Moral motivation is deeply rooted in collective duty, a concept that would be quite foreign to Americans, just as enlightened self-interest does not translate across the Atlantic in the other direction.[56]

We see here the deep effects of welfarism. To the British, the charitable impulse is imbued with the values of the state; in America, it is imbued with the values of the market. In Britain, we regard giving as akin to paying taxes: an unpleasant duty. In America, they regard giving as akin to buying something: a fair exchange in which the expenditure is reciprocated by a benefit. No wonder they give more.

As this suggests, in Britain charitable giving is squeezed out by high taxation. Those worried that lower taxes would prompt selfish, short-term spending rather than philanthropy can rest easy. As Beth Breeze, the left-leaning Deputy Director of the Institute of Philanthropy, puts it, 'tax relief does stimulate spending on public goods rather than on individual consumption'.

America has had tax relief on charitable giving since the 18th century. We have only more recently begun to recognise the need for fiscal incentives: the last Conservative Government introduced payroll and Gift Aid donations, and Labour have removed their upper and lower thresholds, so making all charitable donations eligible for tax benefits. These are welcome

56 Wright, Karen. "Generosity vs. Altru... Philanthropy and Ch... the US and UK." Vol... no. 4 (2002), pp. 3...

reforms, but we could go much further.

The best policy is the simplest. Joseph Leconte's suggestion for reform in the US would work just as well here – and it would help shift our culture of remote altruism to one of local generosity:

> By allowing every family to give a portion of what it owes in taxes to local charities – religious or secular – the state would admit it can't solve every social problem on its own. The essential thing is to reduce public spending by the value of the credit. If – as Bush proposed – the average taxpaying family could direct £500 of its tax bill to private organisations assisting the needy, families would become much more savvy about effective charities in their own neighbourhood. This could help shift responsibility for the poor from distant government bureaucracies to citizens and community-based groups.[57]

The third requirement, after love and money, is time. The decline of voluntary and communal activity in the West has been well documented, by Fukuyama and Robert Putnam among others. There are many proposals for reversing the decline, the best of which – such as David Cameron's suggestion of tying benefit entitlements to voluntary activity – recognise the American insight that altruism responds to incentives, that affection must be tied with interest. In the same spirit, here is

---

America has had tax relief on charitable giving since the 18th century. We have only more recently begun to recognise the need for fiscal incentives: the last Conservative Government introduced payroll and Gift Aid donations, and Labour have removed their upper and lower thresholds.

---

another idea.

It is a staple of the crusty Conservative colonel's analysis of modern Britain that we have suffered from the ending of National Service. A period in the Army gave young boys something to do on leaving school, and made men of them; it gave them a spirit of patriotism and civic duty, and it brought them into contact with their peers from other places and other classes.

The crusty colonel is right. Young men and women from all backgrounds (plebeians are not the only yobs: visit Rock in Cornwall on a Saturday night in summer to see what a public school education can do for your manners) need structure, discipline and a purpose. National service, suitably modernised, has never been more necessary. The traditional 'gap year' is currently the preserve of the lucky few. We should broaden it.

Legislation in this area could address another thorny policy issue: higher education funding. It is right that young people experience a slice of life between school and work: it is not necessarily right that this experience takes place in a university. The government's target of getting 50% of all school leavers into higher education is wrong: too many students simply rack up debt in exchange for a useless and ill-taught degree. Far better to incentivise some form of national service, which could, if the youth desired, qualify him or her for university funding.

New national service would not just mean the Armed Forces. School leavers could apply to spend a year with any organisation which has a public purpose, such as a charity, church or public agency. It might be sensible to restrict the scheme to domestic organisations (if they want to go 'travelling' they can do it in their own time).

Organisations which take gap students would qualify for tax relief, or a grant, and could pay their students a stipend to cover living expenses. Universities would assess applicants on what they had done in their gap year.

Qualitative public opinion surveys show that Conservatives fail to win elections because they lack a moral message – that is, they appear to lack moral integrity. More particularly, the Conservative Party has failed to benefit from the perception, common throughout the western world, that the centre-right stands for the small and local against the big and national. The Tories are seen as even more 'establishment' than Labour.

The two political imperatives for the Tories, therefore, are to moralise and to localise. 'Moralising', of course, does not mean preaching from on high: it means imbuing the Party's message with a moral motif, and celebrating the compassionate instincts of the public. 'Localising' does not mean government abandoning its responsibilities: it means taking direct action to restore to the public their rightful power over the institutions which affect them. An emphasis on civil society will enable this, creating a radical agenda which is bent on creating not wrecking things.

Localisation and moralisation represent the two principles which define Letwin's 'stubborn tension': the freedom principle and the belonging principle. When the Conservative Party is seen simultaneously to address people's 'anger at constriction' and their 'dread of loneliness', and to accommodate these instincts in a coherent and practical philosophy, then they will win again.

Renewing the conversation

Jesse Norman

In the aftermath of the recent London bombings, many public figures including the Prime Minister have declared how vital it is to preserve our 'way of life', our 'culture' or our 'values'. In fighting against terrorism, however, what are we fighting for exactly? If Conservatives can answer this question, they will have gone a long way towards setting out a distinctively Conservative vision for society, and so a political direction for themselves as a party.

One can address this topic, albeit obliquely, by reconsidering a neglected line of thought to be found in the work of the political philosopher Michael Oakeshott. Following Oakeshott, we can distinguish between two rival conceptions of the state. The first is that of the civil state, and sees the state as an association of citizens – that is, of individuals who are formally equal in their rights before the law. As citizens, they are united not by any common purpose or plan but in a shared recognition of a system of rules, and of a single civil authority standing behind those rules.

Compare this view, by contrast, to the state conceived as an enterprise or undertaking in and of itself – not merely as capitalist, or business-friendly, but as a project in its own right. In this case, individuals are not viewed as citizens. Rather, they are seen as contributors to a common undertaking, who come together to promote a recognised set of substantive goals – such as national prosperity, industrial productivity, or cultural or religious unity.

Naturally, each state has rules that constrain its activities, on pain of ungovernability. Yet the nature of the rules is radically different in each case. In a civil state, the rules will tend to be procedural, universal and categorical. The function of government is, on this view, not to do anything as such, it is just to govern. The state has no goals or projects of its own, over and above those of the individuals or groups being governed. Rather, it exists to devise, promulgate and enforce laws by which people may go about their private business in an orderly and secure way; and these laws will themselves thus be enabling and non-instrumental, rather than oriented towards specific social or political ends.

In an enterprise state, on the other hand, the function of government is precisely to achieve certain social, political, religious or other objectives. It can never be content merely to govern – it is, as it were, ambitious. The rules in such a state will thus tend to be purposive, managerial, specific and instrumental in character. Government in an enterprise state can never rest easy, for nothing is ever as good as it could be, and so there will always appear to be scope for government action to improve it. If poverty or economic underperformance or crime exists, it is but a short step for government to be given the task of improving the situation.

These two conceptions are idealised, of course. Neither is, nor ever could be, exemplified in its pure form, and so every actual state has elements or aspects of each. They are, however, distinct, indeed formally exclusive of each other: one is organised under the category of procedure, the other under that of purpose. In short, the two are rivals, struggling over the soul of a given state, forever pulling it in the directions of self-restraint or ambition as each gains or loses the upper hand, in an essential tension.

We can readily see both conceptions at work in the history of British government: the civil state in such things as Magna Carta, due process, and voting rules; the enterprise state in Great Britain Plc, the No. 10 Downing Street 'Delivery Unit', five year plans, public service targets, and the national bid to host the Olympic Games in London.

So why does this distinction matter? First, a factual observation. It will be obvious by now that Britain is increasingly an enterprise state, and not a civil one. Those in authority have never been indifferent to people's economic or social well-being, of course. But for the state itself to be used as economic engine, safety net or service provider is a modern, and specifically 20th Century, innovation. Many would argue that this is a natural political response to factors ranging from the extension of the franchise, through improved communications and greater social awareness, to concern at economic competition. If Great Britain Plc is not well run, with all its resources deployed and its productivity annually increasing, then how can our prosperity be maintained?

But this cheery managerialism has a deep drawback, for the growth of the enterprise state tends always to abridge our freedom before the law. Recall that the enterprise view is one that judges people, not as citizens, but by their contributions to some overarching corporate goal. In such a state, the interests of citizens are always subordinate to the overall project of the state itself. The best citizen is, thus, not a citizen at all, but a Stakhanov: a star worker, a star entrepreneur, or parent, saver, taxpayer. Formal equality is thus replaced by a social metric assessing people by their contributions to the corporate whole; and, often, by a strand of public moralising that seeks to justify these assessments.

Taken to its furthest logical limit, the enterprise state thus results in a kind of fascism, in which all private interests are subordinated to those of the state itself. We can see this in Mussolini's infamous slogan *'Tutto nello Stato, niente al di fuori dello Stato, nulla contra lo Stato'* ('everything in the state, nothing outside the state, nothing against the state'). Or take a perhaps still more notorious example, Hitler's *'ein Volk, ein Reich, ein Fuhrer'* ('one people, one regime, one leader'). This was not merely a call for Germans to associate themselves with a national project incarnated in the leader's own person; it was also a tacit invitation to ignore intermediate institutions or obstructing laws in so doing.

Now the contrast between civil and enterprise is especially relevant to a nation's decision to go to war. For what is war, at root? It is a massive gathering of energies, with the common goal of repelling, subduing or conquering an enemy. This is, of its essence, an enterprise. After a war, the machinery of wartime administration is rarely if ever fully demobilised. And so the decision to go to war generally entails, at the very deepest level, a further, and long-term, move along the spectrum already identified.

In a 'war' on terrorism, something subtly different is taking place. The rhetoric of war preserves a tacit presumption of supreme collective effort, and of the suspension of normal constitutional arrangements. Yet with global terrorism, as the clichÈ goes, there is no theatre of conflict as such, no single command and control structure, no readily identifiable enemy, no obvious end of hostilities. Virtually anything can be a target – think of Beslan – and anyone a foe, and it is in the nature of the 'privatized' terrorism of today that at any given time the true scale of the threat, real or imagined, can never be known.

Yet here again Oakeshott's distinction can help us. First, because we can understand terrorist groups themselves as enterprise associations of a particularly vicious and utopian variety, heedless of the interests and well-being of their members in pursuit of their ultimate goals. And secondly, because it sensitises us to the value of our freedoms as private citizens. One might think that if anything can be a target, the role of the state in protecting its citizens would be a somewhat limited one. Yet faced with unquantifiable terrorist threats, the default response today is to call for more government: more surveillance, more detention of private individuals, more state secrecy. The effect of a war on terrorism is, thus, to institutionalise a targeted country on a 'war' footing, for an extended period, against an undefined threat. It is precisely at such moments that our sensitivity to civil procedure, to constitutional safeguards, and to the basic rights of each citizen as a citizen, should be at its greatest.

Winston Churchill memorably recognized this when he said, on November 21, 1943:

> The power of the Executive to cast a man into prison without formulating any charge known to the law, and particularly to deny him the judgement of his peers, is in the highest degree odious and is the foundation of all totalitarian government whether Nazi or Communist [...]
> Extraordinary power assumed by the Executive should be yielded up when the emergency declines. Nothing is more abhorrent than to imprison a person or keep him in prison because he is unpopular. This is really the test of civilisation.

Now to politics. Why might Churchill take violations of civil rights – even at the height of war – as the real test of civilisation? And what does this line of thought imply for Conservatives reflecting on the state of Britain and British society?

Most notably, it gives point and purpose to the Conservative critique of government interference and micro-management. Our majoritarian model of democracy has historically accorded huge powers to the executive. Over many years, these have been increasingly centralised in Whitehall, away from competing sources of power, notably in local government. At the same time, many of the constitutional safeguards in law and custom that have traditionally legitimated such power have been eroded. Moreover, the general public does not seem willing to note and hold government to account for these changes. On the contrary, it appears less willing either to defer to established authority or – single issue politics apart – to engage in the political process itself.

Within this context, the effect of the Blair/Brown years so far has been, without any doubt, to push the ratchet several further notches over towards an enterprise state. The issue here is not so much the size of the state *per se* or the amount of GDP consumed in taxes, important though these things are. Rather, it concerns the degree to which the state has pervaded the lives, the goals and the motivations of ordinary people. Think of tax credits, which now offer state financial support at the margin for those on three times average income; of pension credit, for which over half of all pensioners will soon be eligible; or of the Home Office's reported plan to target some children

---

Over the past eight years, Conservatives have had to take cold comfort from Mr Blair's committed occupancy of the centre-right in British politics, and Mr Brown's unwillingness to tamper with the structural economic reforms of the Thatcher years.

---

from 'problem homes' as potential criminals from the age of three years.

Over the past eight years, Conservatives have had to take cold comfort from Mr Blair's committed occupancy of the centre-right in British politics, and Mr Brown's unwillingness to tamper with the structural economic reforms of the Thatcher years. Labour has lost, if not yet power, then at least the intellectual argument. But no-one can properly take comfort from this government's continuing, unselfconscious and often utopian extension of state influence over the lives of its citizens.

Nevertheless, if it is not to seem merely partisan, such a critique can only have force in the context of a positive view of British society. Here again, however, I suggest Oakeshott has a persuasive answer: we should think of a society, and specifically of British society, as embodying a distinctive kind of conversation. By this, he means we should recognise it as composed of different traditions, each of which has its own special 'voice' – the voices of science, of business, of religion, of the law, of education, or of the arts, to take only some leading examples. In a conversation, each voice has its own character, yet each must speak in common terms to others if it is to be understood, to move, to persuade, or to command. How they develop, how they play into each other, and how they are heard by different people will determine the character of the conversation as a whole.

The conversational metaphor is a pregnant one, for three reasons. First, any conversation demands a context of mutual respect and order, in short of civility – this is a basic rule of conduct between citizens dealing with each other under the rule of law. In any conversation, all voices have their place; and though they may be ignored once speaking, none is to be forbidden in advance from speaking at all. All are, in effect, regarded as autonomous and individual. Secondly, a vibrant conversation is one whose voices are diverse, mature, self-confident and independent; in short, the voices of citizens, able to examine authority, to question it, and to hold it to account. Thirdly, it is a distinctively European achievement to have first developed the canonical institutions – such as the nation state, the rights of individuals as citizens to speak and associate freely, the marketplace, the political forum – through and between which our cultural conversation takes place, and from which it continues to spread out into the world. And it is this insistence on the acknowledgement of civil authority expressed through the rule of law that specifically differentiates the European tradition from, for example, the Islamic one, in which the demands of law and religion are not merely coextensive and self-reinforcing, but actually identified with each other.

As in conversation, so in a society. When we fight terrorism, to return to my starting question, it is this for which we are fighting. Understanding society as a kind of conversation, however, may strike the reader as fanciful and speculative. On the contrary, I suggest it can be the basis for a vigorous and coherent new Conservatism.

First, the idea of conversation locates the Conservative critique of Labour in exactly the right place. The present government is characterised by a default instinct to extend the powers of the state over the lives of its citizens. In conversational terms, one might think this the analogue of the domineering bore at the table, whose loudness overwhelms the talk of others. A better parallel is that of the patriarch, in whose unspeaking presence others feel robbed of air and automatically fall silent. Similarly, the extension of the state, whatever its short-term attractions, tends to undermine the voices, the energy and the creativity of its citizens. If it is hard to see this now, in part that may be because we have lost sight of how rich and fulfilled all human life has the potential to be.

Second, the idea of conversation can guide us to the right way forward: to trust people, to invest in their virtues and not their faults, and to support and extend the institutions that carry on our distinct traditions as a nation. Indeed, the fundamental theme of respect for individuals as citizens suggests three, rather broad-brush principles for political action:

1. individuals, as citizens, should enjoy a default presumption against state intervention in their lives;
2. where there must be state intervention, political decisions should be taken close to the people they affect; and
3. those taking such decisions should be clearly capable of being held accountable by the citizenry for their actions.

These principles are hardly radical; indeed, they may seem to be just motherhood and apple pie. But they have many policy implications. With the overarching idea of conversation in mind, let me sketch three specific areas in which Conservatives can act on them:

Enfranchise our universities: Tuition fees notwithstanding, British universities are, with one exception, now reliant on the state. The result is, inevitably, a culture of deference to government, unending paperwork and an increasing view of universities within government as educational factories targeted at short-term social and industrial objectives, rather than as free-standing institutions of higher learning.

Conservatives should free our universities from state interference. The idea of an Access Regulator should be discarded and further steps taken to guarantee the complete political neutrality of government research grant making. Consultative plans should be developed by which universities can apply to become independent over a ten- or fifteen-year period with state financial bridging funds, in return for commitments to ensure open access and needs-blind admissions.

Make charitable gifts fully tax-deductible: It is widely held that the UK needs to encourage a greater culture of public service, and private philanthropy can be an important part of this. Where there is a crowding-out effect on private giving by state grant making, the role of the state should be reconsidered, here as elsewhere. But the single step that would achieve most would be to make charitable gifts fully tax-deductible. The present system of Gift Aid is a useful first step, but it is unnecessarily small scale, piecemeal and bureaucratic. It should be replaced by a system in which qualifying charitable donations can be used to write down taxable income by some or all of their value at the end of the tax year.

This would reduce or even remove entirely state involvement in private charitable giving, and flag a public recognition of the not-for-profit sector; it would provide a major incentive to donors to give more; and it would send a clear signal that the active personal involvement of all people in public service and so in mutual support of each other is an expectation on them as citizens, and a crucial means by which they can create value for society as a whole.

Support local government: Local government is as ancient as central government in Great Britain, whose origins date back to the 11th Century. Today, however, it is the creature of our constitutionally unitary state. As a result of decades of centralisation, only 4% of taxation is raised locally, and 75% of local spending is funded from the centre.[58] The result in many places is, again, a culture of deference to central government, low levels of popular civil engagement, and little diversity or innovation.

    Conservatives should act to enfranchise local government. The tax burden should be rebalanced away from the centre and towards local government; rate capping should be removed; control over business rates should be given back to local authorities; and discretionary taxes (such as Green taxes, or congestion charges) should be made exempt from equalisation by central government, so that local authorities can keep the full benefits of them. Ideally, once these arrangements have been allowed to bed down successfully, some means would also be found to give constitutional backing, and so a secure long-term basis in law, to the new settlement.

    These are just three areas in which Conservatives can give citizens their voice, and so strengthen our civil society. But there is one final thought to be drawn out from the idea of conversation. This is simply to remind ourselves of the importance of civility itself as a value in public debate. Conceived as it has been here, a conservative voice is naturally civil; it recognises the right of others to speak; it is confident in its views, and acknowledges what is of value in those of others; it is persuasive, not overbearing; it is restrained in its criticism, and it does not leap to judgement. For Conservatives to find this voice again, as a party, would by itself be a significant, and hugely popular, achievement.

---

58 *Local government in England*, ODPM 20

SMF Publications

Whose Responsibility is it Anyway?
Jessica Asato (ed.)
This collection of essays brings together different perspectives on the public health debate, seeking to find the balance between state intervention and individual responsibility. Published in the lead up to the second White Paper on public health, it considers who should take responsibility for changing public behaviour and when it is legitimate for the state to intervene.
October 2004, £8.00

Reinventing Government Again
Liam Byrne and Philip Collins (eds.)
Ten years had passed since the publication of Osborne and Gaebler's landmark book *Reinventing Government*. Thus, in 2004, the Social Market Foundation commissioned several authors to reflect on the ten principles for entrepreneurial government that were set out in the original.
December 2004, £15.00

Limits of the Market, Constraints of the State: The public good and the NHS
Rt. Hon Dr John Reid MP
In this essay, Dr. John Reid, then Secretary of State for Health, lays out the case for extending patient choice within the NHS. He tackles two misconceptions head-on: the belief that 'choice' is a value solely for those on the ideological right; and the idea that choice is only meaningful within markets where the chooser's own private money is brought to bear.
January 2005, £10.00

Choice and Contestability in Primary Care
Social Market Foundation Health Commission Report 3
This paper examines the case for introducing certain kinds of choice into the primary care sector of the NHS. It describes the evolution of the current PCT structure of primary care and the reasons for thinking that it is theoretically possible for PCTs to improve the quality and cut the costs of service. It also presents

the case for allowing GP practices to choose the PCT to which they wish to belong, explains how this system could operate in practice and considers the limitations of the system.
February 2005, £10.00

News Broadcasting in the Digital Age
Ann Rossiter
Rossiter argues for the introduction of 'genre' licences, providing commercial broadcasters with the opportunity to bid for financial support to provide specific public service broadcasting (PSB) programming, paid for by 'top-slicing' the BBC licence fee. She argues that the switch from analogue to digital broadcasting removes the incentive for commercial broadcasters to make and show PSB content, particularly at peak times.
February 2005, £10.00

The Future of Incapacity Benefit
Report of the Social Market Foundation Seminar of December 2004
Moussa Haddad (ed.)
Figures produced in 2004 show that more than 50 percent of claimants have been on incapacity benefit for more than five years. Drawing on thoughts presented at an SMF seminar, Jane Kennedy, then Minister for Work at the Department for Work and Pensions, outlines the steps government is taking to combat the 'incapacity trap'.
February 2005, £10.00

Too Much, Too Late: Life chances and spending on education and training
Vidhya Alakeson
This report argues that the link between educational attainment and family background will not be broken as long as the pattern of spending on education and training continues to offer a far greater public subsidy to tertiary rather than preschool education. The report proposes a reallocation of spending in the medium term in favour of children under five.
March 2005, £15.00